CONNIE

LETTA
IN
CHINA

GREAT IS THY FAITHFULNESS

Letta in China
by Connie Seaward Ong

Connie Ong © 2000

4th Printing October 2020

SEAWARD
PUBLISHING HOUSE

Seaward Publishing House
17255 139th Pl SE, Renton, WA 98058

Book design by Sharon Tan, Full Bleed Pte Ltd, Singapore

ISBN: 978-0-9995173-2-1

CONTENTS

"A faith affirming, authentic story which inspires a closer walk with God. Profoundly proclaims how one life dedicated to God can impact generations."

Mrs Holly Giffen-Canby, Oregon

"A story that reminds us of God's unfailing love and His faithfulness. My life has forever been impacted by my mother and I know as you read this book your life will never be the same."

Rev Dr Margaret Seaward
~ Daughter of Letta T. Hansen
~ Missionary to Singapore

ACKNOWLEDGEMENTS

T his book was born with the help of so many people, and I would like to acknowledge each one of them for their contributions. Firstly, I would like to acknowledge the late Rev. Andrew Teuber, my grand-uncle, without whom this book would ever have been written. He was Letta's brother and had always felt that there should be a book about her life. He had done some interviews and had about fifty pages of rough manuscript notes which he intended on making into a book. He went to be with Jesus before his dream could be fulfilled, and the notes were handed to my two sisters, Debbie and Pam, before they fell into my hands. I was living in Japan when the notes first came across my desk, and I couldn't escape the deep impression that this book needed to be written. I understood why Uncle Andy wanted this story told; it is a story of God's faithfulness.

I want to thank Dr. Rev. George Wood of the Assemblies of God. In 1996, as General Secretary of the Assemblies of God, Dr. Wood released important photocopied documents from the archives of the Division of Foreign Missions which were invaluable to the research process of this book. May God bless Dr. Wood for his help in releasing the documents so that this book could be written accurately.

Special thanks go to Mary Smalley from the library at the Yale school of Divinity. She helped with the mailing of a copy of the Galt papers. The papers were essential in researching the internment years of Letta T. Hansen.

My mother, Rev. Dr. Margaret Seaward, has to receive very special thanks simply for the fact she has been a most wonderful mother. I would also like to thank her for the countless times she shared with me stories of her mother. Thank you, Mom, for your willingness to sacrifice time from your busy schedule to read through the manuscript to make sure everything was accurately recorded.

I want to thank my late father, Rev. Dr. Fred O. Seaward Jr., for being willing to write the foreword for this book. I know how busy my father was and yet he took time to write this for me. I am thankful to my father for his love of books and writing that he passed on to me. If not for the countless volumes of classical literature in the back room of our family's home I may never have found the love of the written page.

My late Uncle Harold answered question upon question from me in regards to his memories of his mother. Thank you to Vicki, his daughter, who patiently wrote out all the answers for her father and sent them to me in Africa via email.

I must thank my dearest husband for his encouragement during this time of researching and writing the book. My dear children deserve an award for their patience with me as I would 'get lost' in the researching or the writing of the book.

Above all, I must thank God for His love and mercy. I thank Him for the continued strength to finish this project. His faithfulness has made this story possible.

Connie Ong

FOREWORD

For many years the seeds of this book were sown in the hearts of a number of people. The first to make mention of this was Evangelist Andrew Teuber, the younger brother of Letta. He was the pastor of the church in Omak, Washington when Grandma and Grandpa Hansen and their three children, Gwendolyn,

Harold Jr., and Margaret Belle, returned from China in the second prisoner of war exchange with Japan.

I'm not exactly sure when or where this idea was birthed in Uncle Andy's heart, but I remember him talking excitedly about the concept of a book written about Letta and her life's story and experiences. When he visited Singapore with Uncle Wayne (Rev. Wayne Ridout, husband of Faith, Grandma Hansen's younger sister), he talked about his sister's life and the fact that others should know about it. I can still clearly remember that momentous visit to his home in Springfield, Missouri, when he took out the materials of the beginnings of a manuscript. He interviewed Margaret Belle, my wife and Letta's youngest daughter. Later he realized that he would not be able to complete the task so he passed it on to my eldest daughter Debbie Rae Morris, of Tulsa, Oklahoma. Although well qualified and very capable to accomplish this task, her family and work obligations hindered her from being able to work on it. Thus the task of research, compilation, and composition of the book fell to my youngest daughter, Connie Seaward Ong, a missionary to Ghana, West Africa. She took on the assignment even though she had been only about 5 years old when Letta went to her much-deserved home in heaven to be with her blessed Lord and Savior.

I believe this book has been brought forth as a result of prayer, tears, and of course much labor. As a result it will speak deeply to the hearts and lives of all those who read it. Letta was a woman who was sold out to God. She never lost the heart of giving from the time that she was a youth until she laid her banner down. Although in actuality she was my mother-in- law, to me she was always more like a mother. I can still hear her soft voice saying, "Now, Margie" or "Now, Fred." How I cherish the few times we had together and especially the last couple years of her life with us in Singapore.

I recall the time when she was recovering from a serious heart attack; she was resting in her room one day when a young man (who is now a pastor in Singapore) came for a Bible study lesson with Grandma Hansen. I met him at the door and apologized to him, telling him that Grandma was too ill to meet with him that day. She overheard me from the back room and called out, "Is that George? Please send him back to me." That was Letta.

Letta was saved, baptized in the Holy Spirit, and called to the ministry at a very young age, and I'm sure her story will challenge all who read it, young and old alike. I felt honored to be invited to write the foreword of this book, and it has given me the greatest pleasure to do so. I sincerely believe that through it many will not only be called, but will step out and respond in answer to that call. May you find in this book a very personal message from the Lord directly to you that will cause you to walk worthy of the message and calling of His precious servant, Letta.

In His Great Service,
Rev. Dr. Fred Seaward
Senior Pastor
Elim Assembly of God Church
Singapore

1

Twenty-two-year-old Letta Teuber pressed her 4'11" frame up against the railing of the S.S. Persia. She strained to see if she could catch one last glimpse of her cousin as the ship pulled away from the San Francisco docks. Standing there on the deck of the huge vessel, she felt as though her heart was being cut up in a dozen pieces. With a quick sweep of her hand she whisked a tear off her cheek and replaced a strand of her auburn hair back into the bun on top of her head.

The pounding of her heart deafened her; trembling, she clung onto the railing. Closing her eyes, her thoughts focused on where she was going and where she had been. On this day, March 11, 1920, she stood on the threshold of the rest of her life.

The past two months held so many good-byes, and now once again she was saying "Good-bye." But this time, it seemed so final.

When would she be able to see the land of her birth? When could she visit once again with her beloved family? How could she make it all the way to China, on her own? The questions came fast and furiously, causing her head to ache. But as quickly as the questions came, a peace descended upon her, removing the pain of each query.

Her mind began to focus on the One who had led her thus far. Surely, her Jesus, her dearest and closest companion would be with her now. Hadn't

He promised that He would never leave nor forsake her?

Leaning against the railing of the S.S. Persia, Letta allowed her mind to wander back in time. She could see how everything in her life had been directing her to this very moment in time. Her heavenly Father had ordered her footsteps from the time she was a child. Actually, the more she contemplated it; she had to admit her steps were laid out from before her birth.

Her father, Adolph Teuber, had been a Congregational minister in Antelope County, Nebraska, U.S.A. He married one of his parishioners, a young lady named Annie Irene Mum. The couple moved to Hebron, North Dakota, where Pastor Teuber was in charge of another Congregational church.

One week, while he was preparing for his Sunday address, Pastor Teuber discovered, as Martin Luther had once discovered, that he had to accept Christ by faith alone. He bowed his head right there in the middle of his sermon preparation and gave his heart to Jesus. His life was never to be the same again.

While in North Dakota, the Teuber family grew to include eleven children. In the year 1898, on April 14th, Letta became the third of these children. As she grew up, she was constantly exposed to the teachings of God. Her father raised her to love the Word of God and the things of God.

In the year 1906, Adolph Teuber felt impressed to move his family to the state of Washington. Upon their arrival, they discovered a great revival in progress. A minister by the name of Reverend Gurley was conducting special meetings in a large auditorium, where services continued three times a day, every day of the week — and this had been going on for two years!

The Teubers found this all very new and exciting. They yearned for what they saw at the meetings, and as a result, God brought them into the light and knowledge of His Holy Spirit and His ministry. During these meetings, Letta, then just 8 years old, received the baptism of the Holy Spirit. She lay pros- trate before the Lord for hours; she would receive wonderful words from God and beautiful visions. On one of these occasions Letta saw herself preaching to a sea of children in China, pointing them to the way of salvation. Many of the children in the vision received Jesus as their personal savior. When she opened her eyes that day, she knew without a doubt the call of God on her life: that she must be focused on getting herself to China.

From that point on, everything she did or thought was geared towards her being able to leave for China. Now the day had finally arrived for her departure. She opened her eyes and glanced out over the sea of people who were on the docks singing as the ship continued to pull away. She knew that although she felt emotional pain at this moment, she was going in the direction that God had planned for her. She would not need to fear nor dread, for surely He would go before her and prepare the way.

The pain of parting seemed too great to bear. It had only been two months earlier, on January 24, 1920, that she left her family in Washington State. What a parting that had been! She could remember standing at the railroad station with her family and friends, hugs and kisses abounding, as everyone was eager to let her know that she would be greatly missed. She couldn't bear the finality of saying good- bye to those who had nurtured and inspired her over the years.

When she boarded the train, the group sang the song "God be with you 'til we meet again," and as the song drifted through the air, she could see her parents' eyes welling up with tears. She reached in for her little white handkerchief and put it to the corner of her eye where a tear was forming. She knew she was doing the right thing, but her heart felt torn with emotions.

The months of January through March of that year were spent saying good-bye too many times. Each place she stopped along the way, whether to minister in a church or just to rest before the next leg of the journey, she met people and then had to end up saying good-bye. She felt so alone, and yet in those times of feeling alone, she realized all the more that her Jesus would never leave her. She knew that Jesus loved her and cared for her, and now she must lean hard on Him. He was the only one who could take care of her.

That old familiar song, "God be with you 'til we meet again," was being sung by those on the shore, and the sound of their sweet voices jolted her back to the present. The words of the song seeped into the depths of her soul. Letta smiled as she felt her spirit soar, slowly at first and then with more strength and power. Like an eagle her spirit rose steadily higher and higher.

She whispered, "Thank you Father, for I never have to say goodbye to You! You are with me wherever I go. You never leave me nor forsake me. I can lean on You, and surely You will take care of my every footstep. Thank you!"

She turned to go to her cabin with a sense of peace that surpassed human understanding, warming her innermost being. Entering the 6' by 8' cabin, she met her travel companions, Rev. and Mrs. Harold Hansen. Suitcases and steamer trunks crammed the stuffy room, leaving barely enough space to walk. Letta took stock of the small room and wondered how she and the Hansens were going to survive the long voyage to China. How thankful she was to this wonderful couple who had so graciously allowed her to travel with them all the way to China.

The Hansens had only known her for a short time. They had come one Sunday to hold a missionary meeting in Letta's church, the First Assembly of Tacoma. In the midst of the service, God spoke specifically to Letta and told her He wanted her to go to China with the Hansens.

She responded, "Lord, if this is really You speaking to me, let Sister Hansen come and tell me that she feels You want me to go with them."

At the close of the service, Letta made her way to the door of the church. Sister Hansen stopped her and asked her if God had ever spoken to her about going to China. Letta responded by telling Sister Hansen that God had spoken to her in that very meeting. Sister Hansen confirmed what Letta shared, and thus the decision was made to journey together to China. Now here she was in this tiny cabin with these two wonderful people.

She squeezed herself past the trunks and went towards the bunk bed. The bed looked like it was made of hard planks. With the lack of windows and proper ventilation, the heat in the cabin was almost suffocating. Letta gave Margaret Hansen a weak smile. Sister Hansen encouraged Letta to sit down for a while.

"Oh, I don't feel much like sitting," Letta responded. "But I would appreciate it if you and Rev. Hansen would pray for me. For I feel as though this parting has been a bit much for me."

The Hansens stood next to her and prayed over her. She felt her spirit lift once again as the prayer ended.

"Come to supper, Letta." Sister Margaret Hansen urged, "You will feel better once you have something hot inside you."

Letta shook her head, responding quickly, "Oh, no. You both go on without me. I feel as though I cannot eat right now. I'll just stay in the cabin and sort through some of my things."

The Hansens pushed their way past the trunks and squeezed through the door. Once they had left, Letta was able to prepare herself for bed. Changing into her nightclothes proved to be no easy feat. Clambering up to the top bunk, she adjusted herself on the plank bed. Moving from side to side, Letta fought to find a position that would bring a bit of comfort to her sleep. After much tossing and turning she finally realized there was to be no comfort on this hard bunk. At long last, sleep overpowered even the need for comfort, and she fell into a deep slumber.

Despite the hard bunk, Letta awoke the next morning in better spirits. Her eyelids fluttered open and she looked drowsily at the ceiling.

The ship tossed to and fro, making it feel as though it would turn over at any moment. Letta could not pay attention to the waves or even to the lack of comfort in the cabin, because all she could think of was her growling stomach. She quickly dressed to go down to breakfast, leaving the Hansens alone in the cabin so they would have a chance to get up and prepare themselves for the day as well.

Breakfast proved to be wonderful. With her stomach now full, Letta walked out onto the deck and watched the waves crashing against the ship. The ocean spray dusted her cheeks as she leaned over the railing and looked out at the dark colors of the ocean. Her mind couldn't help but think of her heavenly Father, for hadn't He created this magnificent wonder? He created the waves, and He could also still the waves! This marvelous God chose to love her with an undying love. The thought of His love overpowered her.

Letta moved away from the railing and sat down on a deckchair. She pulled out her little devotional, Quiet Talks on Prayer. She flipped to the first page and began to read slowly, digesting each and every word. After some time, she put the book down and picked up her Bible. As she continued to read, she felt the strength of God coming into her, and she knew that no matter what may cross her path, her Father would be there to strengthen her and uphold her with His right arm. He indeed was faithful!

Letta spent most of her days on deck studying her Bible, practicing her guitar, and learning the Chinese language. The ship came into some rough waters towards the end of the first week. Waves dashed high over the railings, and at one point, the waves poured right into the dining room portals, drenching many of the people there. The tossing and turning of the ship caused the excitement level of the passengers to increase. The rough water beat against the ship smashing three lifeboats into pieces. All the decks were flooded and many dishes were broken. Every time a large wave crashed against the ship, people were dashed about and a chorus of screams arose. The possibility of the ship sinking plagued many of the passengers' minds.

During the night of the storm, as Letta drifted in and out of sleep, the ship suddenly lurched onto its side, causing Sister Hansen to scream so loudly that the sound reverberated throughout the cabin.

"Sister Hansen, are you alright?" Letta called out nervously.

There was no response. Soft sobs filled the dark cabin. She could hear Rev. Hansen quietly consoling his wife.

Letta spoke again, "Sister Hansen, just imagine that you are in a cradle and you are being rocked to sleep. God is rocking us all to sleep."

There was silence, but then she heard Margaret Hansen say, "Thank you, I feel much better now. Thank you for your kind words of comfort."

Indeed, Letta slept like a baby that night. She felt as though she was in Her Father's arms. There was no need to fear, because whatever He had planned for her would be in her best interest. She could rest in that assurance.

The next morning she awoke early and scurried down to take a bath. It turned out to be a very cold and salty bath. She shivered as she dressed herself, thinking with certainty that she probably wouldn't be taking too many more of these cold baths! As she left the bathroom, a wave splashed over the railing and almost knocked her over. Letta knew she had nothing to fear. Her God had delivered her in the past, and she knew He had the ability to deliver her again!

In previous years when she'd been working to support the family, she had to take a trolley car to and from work. One winter evening she had to travel home in the darkness. Her home was situated in a very deserted and lonely area, far from the main road. As she approached her stop, Letta rang the bell to signal she wished to disembark. When the trolley stopped, she stood up, and to her surprise a man got up and came behind her, taking her arm. He said, "Let me help you. A young lady should not be alone."

Letta stiffened and said, "I am alright. I can take care of myself."

But the man held her elbow firmly and steered her forward. "Well, I am going to help you," he responded roughly.

Letta prayed silently in her heart. They approached a deserted house, and he pushed her to go down the path towards the old deserted building. She forced herself to speak calmly as she said, "This is NOT where I live!"

"Well, this is where we are going!" The man said.

Chills ran up and down Letta's spine. She cried out to the Lord in her heart, praying, "Father, HELP me, oh HELP me!!"

As soon as the prayer went up, she heard a whirring sound. She realized that an angel was present between her and this man! All fear left her as she proclaimed loudly, "Oh, THERE he is!"

Alarmed and confused, the man stopped in his tracks, looking around wildly, demanding, "WHO... there who is?"

Looking straight into the man's eyes, Letta responded calmly, "Why don't you know? The angel of the Lord is here!!"

Instantly he dropped her arm and fled as if someone or something was chasing him. At that moment Psalm 34:7 became a reality to Letta: *The Lord saves those who fear Him. His angel camps around them.*

After the fury of the storm was over, calm weather prevailed and the days continued to roll by, slowly and without much event. As the weather became warmer, Letta found herself up on deck more than in the cabin. The stuffiness of the cabin was too much for her to bear. The ship stopped briefly at Honolulu and then went on to China from there, journeying out once again across the waters.

Letta felt anxious to get to her destination. She wanted so much to be able to start the work that the Lord had laid out for her to do. But she took the time on the long passage to pray and contemplate everything that God had told her. She wanted to be sure that when she got to China, she would not only be ready physically for God's service, but also spiritually and emotionally.

One day as Letta sat up on the deck, meditating on the goodness of God, her mind wandered back to the time she had helped to start a Sunday school in Lemon Beach, Washington. Although the task seemed too great for such a young lady to bear, she had dutifully followed the Lord's leading and taken up the job He had laid before her. On one occasion, there were several people gathered together who were praying for this Sunday school and each of its members. During their prayer time, Letta lifted her eyes to see a divine figure enter the room. He moved gently through the midst of the people gathered there, laying His hand upon each person's head. Letta wept as she recognized that it was indeed her Lord and Master mercifully visiting this humble prayer meeting. Now looking out across the vast sea she couldn't help but be reminded of Isaiah 40:10-12

"Behold, the Lord God will come with might, with His arm ruling for Him. Behold, His reward is with Him, And His recompense before Him. Like a shepherd He will tend His flock, In His arm He will gather the lambs, and carry them in His bosom; He will gently lead the nursing ewes. Who has measured the waters in the hollow of His hand, and marked off the heavens by the span, and calculated the dust of the earth by the measure, and weighted the mountains in a balance, and the hills in a pair of scales?"

Yes, the Lord is mighty, she thought to herself. Looking out across the waters, no one could doubt His vast strength and greatness. Didn't the verse say these great waters could be measured in the hollow of His hand? Oh, yes! But what thrilled her more, as she meditated on these verses, was that this mighty God was gentle. Like a shepherd, He would choose to gather

His lambs to His bosom. The knowledge of her great God and Creator overwhelmed Letta. She knew, in her heart, that just as surely as she had seen His divine presence with her that night in Lemon Beach, so He was with her now.

The ship finally reached Japan, their stopping-off point until they could continue on to China. A foggy morning greeted them when they pulled into the harbor. After getting her things together, Letta waited for the doctor and the customs officials to process her so that she could go ashore. Finally at 3.30 pm, she stepped on shore and felt such a relief to be standing on dry ground once again! On March 30, 1920, she was standing on Japanese soil.

The rain poured down unmercifully, and all around she could see nothing but large umbrellas and bare feet. The streets, full of mud, appeared very narrow and apparently there were no sidewalks. How strange and new everything was to her.

Someone from the mission came to the dock to welcome Letta and the Hansens. He drove them up to the home of Vera and Ralph Collier, Letta's missionary friends. Letta was thrilled to see them; finally, a familiar face from home, and although she was in Japan, a land she had never seen before, she felt content to be fellowshipping with someone from home. She didn't want to admit just how much "home" was tugging at her heart.

The Hansens had told Letta that they would have to remain in Japan until they could find a way to make passage to China. Although Letta was anxious to reach her final destination, she thankfully accepted the fact that they would be here on dry ground for a while longer.

Each day afforded new experiences, learning new ways of doing things. The Japanese houses fascinated Letta, with their entrance areas giving space for shoes to be taken off and slippers to be put on. The doors all seemed much lower than she was used to, but it wasn't an inconvenience for her since her height was only 4'11" anyway! Each house was fitted with sliding doors, and each door was made out of paper.

Letta wasted no time with simply staying at home. She knew this might be her only visit to Japan, so she decided she wanted to see as much of this fascinating country as she could. She and Vera Collier traveled to Tokyo, and it was a good thing that Vera could speak a bit of Japanese, because otherwise their trip would have been impossible since all signs were written in Japanese. Letta wondered how any foreigner would be able to travel if they didn't know the language in this country. This caused her to realize that she must speed up her language lessons, so that when she arrived in China she would not have much difficulty traveling and communicating with the people there.

One evening a couple of Japanese girls came over to the mission house to talk with the missionaries. Letta enjoyed watching as the missionaries took out their Japanese Bibles and shared the good news of Jesus in Japanese. As the time of sharing ended in prayer, Letta couldn't help but notice how bright the Japanese girls' faces had become! They were thrilled to have heard the wonderful story of Jesus and His love for them.

After the prayer time, the small group gathered around for a light Japanese meal and the traditional tea. Letta could tell that the girls were enjoying themselves, and she wanted to join in the conversation too, so she asked one of the missionary ladies to translate for her so that she could be a part of the fellowship.

After the girls had gone, the missionaries asked Letta to share more about her experiences. As she began to share with them, her tiredness left and she felt her spirit being lifted up! Oh, the joy of talking about her Father and Friend!! Finally, at one o'clock in the morning, she stopped and said, "We really must be heading for bed, as tomorrow I have to travel."

Although none wanted their time together to end, everyone agreed that they must indeed get to sleep. They said goodnight to each other for the last time. And as Letta went to her room, she thought, "Once again I have to say goodbye."

Early the next morning Letta arose and prepared to leave. The train for Kobe would leave in the evening, and she had much to do before the departure. It seemed almost impossible to get a simple task done! But God helped her in everything that needed to be accomplished. Her heart raced as she realized that she was heading out for the final leg of her journey!

After what seemed like an interminably long wait, Letta and the Hansens boarded the train and were assigned a sleeper car. By 8am the next morning they had reached Kobe, where they disembarked to give their legs some exercise before continuing on the long train ride. After traveling south throughout the entire day, by 9pm that night they had reached Shimoneseki; from this point in their journey they would continue on to China by steamer ship.

Although Letta dreaded the thought of another steamer trip, she rejoiced at the knowledge that it was bringing her that much closer to the place God had set before her. This trip had taught her much about the true meaning of patience: waiting for God to do things in His perfect timing, and not being anxious or afraid of what would lie ahead.

Thinking back on the events of her journey so far, Letta could clearly see how God had proved to be her provider from the beginning of the trip. When she left her family in Washington, she only had enough money for the passage to China. As she journeyed down towards San Francisco, God had provided her every need. He had gone before her and spoken to many saints to put love offerings into her hands. She knew that now He would go before her and prepare her footsteps, and that all she had to do was follow in obedience to His every word. So, as Letta looked out over the railing of the steamer, she bravely said farewell to the land of Japan, and expectantly turned her face towards her destiny, the beckoning land of China!

As the steamer neared the coast of China, Letta felt a surge of thrilling expectancy. Although she had never been to this land, she felt such a love well up within her for the land and the people. Letta leaned hard against the railing, attempting to get a better view of the country. She felt her heart bursting, but this time it was bursting not with sorrow and sadness, but with joy and gladness! She could hardly contain herself as she saw the view in front of her, a view so foreign and different from any she had ever seen, and yet a sight that reminded her of many visions that the Lord had given her previously. An all-encompassing sense of peace flooded her, for she knew she was coming "home." Now the goodbyes were over at last, and with each step from the first moment her foot touched Chinese ground she would be welcoming new things, new places, and new people in her life.

2

L etta stepped off the train into a crowd of Chinese Christians. The people surged forward surrounding Letta and the Hansens with rejoicing and joyful weeping as they emerged from the train. Letta moved forward smiling and shaking hands with each and every person in the crowd. New, strange names, tossed her way, swirled aimlessly about in her head. No matter how different their names or their appearances were, there was no mistaking the joy that shone from each face.

Their bags and traveling containers were quickly piled high in several wheelbarrows. The Chinese Christians eagerly directed Letta to an awaiting rickshaw. Out from nowhere a small wooden stool appeared and was set strategically in front of the rickshaw, and her newfound friends eagerly pushed her up onto the red brocade seat.

She sat gingerly at the edge of the seat and almost flew off backwards when the rickshaw owner raised the wooden poles to start his run. Letta bounced up and down on the seat as they traveled down the road towards the mission house. At first she tried to take in the new sights surrounding her, but after awhile she just closed her eyes and leaned back on the seat. The rhythmic sound of the rickshaw owner's feet slapping against the ground blended with the steady creaking of the rickshaw's wooden wheels. Letta found herself being lulled to sleep.

The first few days in China went by like a whirlwind. Letta busied herself with getting settled into her new life. As she went about her day, she found herself stopping to inspect everything. The vegetation, the houses, and the roads all looked so different from what she was used to. She wanted to take time to get used to every part of this new home of hers.

Letta continued to study the language with diligence. It was not long before her efforts paid off, and she began to communicate with the Chinese people. Letta practiced speaking Mandarin with anyone who would take the time to talk to her. She felt such excitement the first time she was able to share with some Chinese women about the love of Jesus in her new tongue. Now that she had become proficient in the language she was asked to take over the Sunday school work at the mission.

The children at the Sunday school helped to improve her Mandarin. The children were never embarrassed to let her know when she was making a mistake. When she would say something using the wrong inflection or tone, the children squealed with delight. Letta would stop and ask them what was so funny and they would patiently explain her error. She thanked God for these wonderful teachers.

Her ministry amongst the children was not limited to the church building. Each day she left the house with a teaching scroll tucked under her arm. As she walked along the dirt roads, children ran after her, greeting her excitedly, for they knew why she had come to them. After setting up her things, she would turn and find the children waiting expectantly for her to start teaching.

The story of Jesus and His love became real to those children as she turned each sheet of paper on her teaching scroll. At the end of the teaching time, Letta called out,"Does anyone want this Jesus whom I have told you about to come into your heart?"

Little hands flew up in the air, and the children jumped up and down excitedly saying, "Yes, we want this! We want Jesus!"

It thrilled her heart to see one child after another receiving the precious love of Jesus. Not only did she see them saved, but after their salvation experiences she would see them take a step further and marvelously receive the baptism of the Holy Spirit, just as she herself had received it as a little girl.

The children burst forth into beautiful heavenly languages, languages they did not know. They began to speak in a new tongue, just as the scriptures mention in Acts 2:4:

"And they were all filled with the Holy Spirit and began to speak with other tongues, as the Spirit was giving them utterance."

Once while Letta prayed for the children, some of those scattered throughout the group spoke in clear English. They did not know a word of English, but here they were speaking in clear and correct English. Letta stood amazed at this and listened to hear what they were saying. Each and every one of those children who spoke in English was giving praises to God. They were glorifying the Lord Jesus Christ. They were exalting the King of kings! Letta wept with sheer joy at the wonder of it all.

She remembered the vision God had given her while she was still just a little girl growing up in Washington. In that vision she had seen herself preaching to a sea of children, pointing them to the way of salvation. And now as she stood amongst these children, listening to them glorifying God, she realized that vision was now being fulfilled! What God had promised her years ago — what He had laid out for her years ago — He now had brought to full completion!

Along with her ministry to the children, Letta Teuber helped the Hansens in any way that she could. Many times this just meant accompanying Mrs. Hansen on one of her visitations to the church members. She did each task with a heart of expectation, because she felt privileged to be allowed to serve God in this country! Although thoughts of home would often tug at her heart, her joy in serving her Father in heaven seemed to override any other thought.

She was privileged to see miracles taking place; God had put a special anointing on Rev. Hansen in praying for the sick. A Chinese lady had been brought to the mission in critical condition. The ceiling of her kitchen had collapsed, causing a heavy beam to strike her on her head. Rev. Hansen laid hands on her and prayed for her healing, and she was instantly made whole.

The story of this miracle spread and many more came to know Jesus through the testimony. People would come and see the lady who had been healed, her face shining as she told of God's goodness and mercy to her. There could be no doubt about the healing because her head bore the deep marks from the accident, and the hair never did grow back to cover the scars. Seeing the marks left from the accident, people knew that ONLY God could have caused her to survive.

Healings and miracles continued, and more souls were brought into the Kingdom. Within two months of arriving in China, Letta rejoiced to see a total of sixteen new converts being baptized in water. She marveled at how they stepped down into the water with faces aglow, ready to die to the things of this world, and then rise up out of the water in the newness of life in Christ. Their decision to follow Jesus was not taken lightly; they had to face great persecution from their family members. Despite the fact that they knew the persecution would increase after the baptism, they went into the waters with gladness of heart.

In Letta's Sunday school there were four boys from a Muslim family, and Letta knew that they faced a lot of persecution when they went home from the services each Sunday. The eldest son fell ill from diphtheria, and he was at death's door when the family brought him to Rev. Hansen for prayer. They had heard of the miracles happening at the church and they were desperate for a miracle. God miraculously healed the boy, and as a result the entire family accepted the Lord as their Savior.

Each new day brought unexpected blessings for Letta. She could see God's hand of mercy at work in every situation in her life. God began to expand her ministry beyond the children to even working with the women in the city. Sister Hansen and Letta were frequently invited to their homes to teach them from the Bible. They were elated to have this opportunity to share the Word of God.

God was breaking across all lines and barriers. He brought favor with the Metropolitan Police force, and members of the force came to experience new life in Jesus. As a result of the police officers getting saved, Rev. Hansen was able to make inroads into the prisons to start a new ministry.

On the one hand Letta saw miracles and new roads of ministry opening up for her and the Hansens. On the other hand, Letta could see deep unrest in China. Politically speaking there was a lot of turmoil; fighting continued to rage between the Chinese warlords. Aside from the political unrest, other natural disasters plagued the nation of China.

Floods wiped out the greater part of the grain in the fields and most of the cotton fields were destroyed. This was particularly devastating, because the Chinese people needed the cotton to pad their coats for winter. The rivers had washed out the bridges, thus causing the transportation of heating coal impossible. Letta knew her first winter in China would be difficult, yet she also knew that no matter what the situation, Her God would be by her side. He would go before her, and He would never allow her to endure anything that she could not bear. With that assurance in her heart, she set her face to the future and continued to work faithfully for her Master.

The winter was indeed cold and cruel, just as Letta had anticipated. The believers joined together to help each other in every way they could. The New Year didn't offer any new hope. God was the only hope the Christians in China had, because everything around them was failing. The fierce fighting continued causing food supplies to decrease. Despite the natural circumstances, God continued to rule and reign.

By January 15, 1921, Letta saw nine more souls baptized into the kingdom. The missionaries continued relentlessly to share the gospel wherever they went. Everywhere she went, Letta saw more souls being ushered into the kingdom of God.

The famine conditions worsened and a fund was set up to help the people. Funds were sent from the Assemblies of God in the United States to help those who were starving. The missionaries worked night and day to make sure the funds were properly channeled so as to best benefit the people. They traveled to over thirty villages, searching for those who were in the greatest need of food.

Letta's daily routine was drastically altered by the tragedy that was playing out around her. She and the other missionaries traveled from village to village helping to distribute the grain and collecting names of more people who needed assistance.

Nothing in her life could have prepared her for the pitiful living conditions of the villagers. The moment she entered a village she was besieged by people begging for food. She squeezed her way through people so desperate with hunger they had lost all desire to worry about trying to "save face." They were barely surviving on cakes made with roots of grass and shrubs mixed together with the tops of sweet potatoes. As a result of poor nutrition, the villagers' physical health continued to deteriorate.

At the end of each day, Letta stumbled into her room barely able to muster enough strength to clean herself off. Wiping away the dust and the grime, she attempted to wash away the sad faces she had seen throughout the day. At times she didn't even have the heart to eat, but she knew she had to keep up her strength so that she could help those who were suffering. She flopped onto her bed, her heart heavy with the suffering she had seen. Her only place of solace was in the quiet times she spent with her Savior. She found hope for the days ahead of her, knowing Her God would be faithful to supply the needs of these people.

Each day seemed to dawn a little earlier, and there were more people to attend to. Large quantities of food needed to be organized and distributed. Aside from taking care of the physical needs of those in the villages, Letta had to get back to attending to some of her other duties. She found that as long as she kept her eyes on the Lord, He would keep her full of joy. The joy of the Lord became her source of continual strength.

The mission workers shared the love of God with all the suffering ones. As a result of their efforts, over 7,000 people were fed and taken care of during this terrible famine.

One day in the midst of the famine, the Hansens were summoned to pray for a girl in the early hours of the morning. Letta went with the Hansens to pray for a girl who was possessed with demons. High-pitched screams could be heard coming from the house where the girl was.

The entire household was in an uproar when the missionaries arrived to pray over the girl. They joined together and commanded the demons to get out. For a short time the young girl quieted down and appeared to be coming to herself. Then suddenly, without warning, the girl's body gyrated and blood-curdling screams rose from her throat.

Letta bowed her head and prayed quietly as Rev. Hansen moved forward to command the demons to leave. The little girl's body went limp, falling back onto her bed. A look of peace flooded her face and she smiled at those who had come to pray for her. The demons were gone and the girl and her entire family came to know that God was the true and living God. As time went on, the hidden result of the famine became evident: diseases spread like wildfire, and much to everyone's horror there was an outbreak of Typhus fever.

Letta and Sister Hansen had just come home from another exhausting day, and before they had a chance to rest they were informed that one of the women in the church had contacted Typhus fever. They rushed out the door and down the road to the lady's home.

They were quickly ushered straight into the woman's bedroom, and Letta was shocked to see that she was right at death's door. They prayed for her and then nursed her suffering as best they could. The woman completely recovered soon after they had prayed for her, and those in her house were overjoyed at God's goodness.

Over the next few days the dreadful epidemic found its way right into the mission house. Many of the Christian brothers and sisters fell ill, and now Sister Hansen busied herself running about taking care of their physical needs while praying for them unceasingly.

As it turned out, the Hansens didn't escape the sickness; as soon as the majority of the others gained their health, the Hansens fell ill. Letta was left to try and take care of them. Rev. Hansen looked like he was going to lose his life, but then suddenly he regained his strength. Sister Hansen's body had been run down with all the hard work of caring for those who were sick. She didn't have the strength to fight the disease. Her fever escalated dramatically causing chills to shake her entire body.

Letta stayed by her bedside day and night, helping her in her time of need.

If she heard Margaret Hansen moaning or moving, she wearily laid a damp towel on her burning forehead. She piled blankets on Sister Hansen when she began to shiver uncontrollably.

Letta watched helplessly as Sister Hansen's strength seeped away with each passing day; no amount of medication or aid changed her condition. Rev. Hansen, still weak from his bout of illness, went into the sick room and prayed over his wife. Letta stood away from the bed as he attempted to talk to his wife, but she was unable to respond. He turned and saw Letta watching him.

"My wife is so precious to me, Sister Teuber. She is the one who prayed many years for me to become a Christian."

Letta nodded encouragement; she knew he needed to talk to someone. He continued.

"She would organize prayer meetings in the house, and when the people would come they tried to talk to me but I was a stubborn man, I was! I didn't want to hear about Jesus or anything that He had done. It made me so angry at the time, because I thought she was being fooled by those people."

Rev. Hansen paused and brushed his wife's cheek.

Letta waited quietly for him to continue his story. "One day when those people had come for the prayer meeting, they handed me a tract as they were leaving. I wanted to throw it away as soon as they put it in my hand, but something inside me urged me to read it. That was the day God stopped me in my tracks. When I read the words on that piece of paper, they became alive to me, and from that day on I chose to take Jesus as my personal Savior."

His eyes glistened with tears as he finished his story. Letta's heart went out to Rev. Hansen, for she could see that he longed to see his wife healed so that she could join him again in the ministry that God had set before them.

Although Rev. Hansen wanted to see his wife restored to good health, she continued to deteriorate. Her body, ravished by fever, fought against the suffering she was going through. As she tossed about vigorously in the bed, Letta would reach over and hold her down to keep her from harming her own body. In her delirious state she would cry out and say things that made no sense at all. All the while Letta prayed over her and tried to the best of her abilities to calm the sick woman.

For more than two weeks Letta diligently nursed Sister Hansen, and often she would sleep with her head resting on the edge of the bed where Sister Hansen lay. Early on Easter Sunday morning a sudden movement caused Letta to lift up her head and notice that Sister Hansen's eyelids were attempting to open. She reached feebly for Letta's hand. Grasping her hand, she whispered weakly, "Promise me something."

Letta bent forward, attempting to hear what Sister Hansen was trying to say.

"What do you want me to promise you?" Letta asked.

Breathless, Mrs. Hansen labored on, "Please... promise me...you will take care...of Harold."

Letta pulled her hand away, wondering why Sister Hansen would be asking her to take care of her husband! Composing herself she leaned forward again, assuming that once again Sister Hansen must be delirious.

Patting her hand, Letta said gently, "There, there, you rest now. Try not to worry about your husband. He will be just fine. You must get better now; that is all that matters."

Nothing Letta said could soothe Sister Hansen or keep her from trying to speak. She searched once again for Letta's hand, and with all her strength she repeated, "Please, please! ... Promise me!" Her voice was filled with desperation.

Confused by this strange request, Letta didn't know what to do. She knew she had to calm her patient, so she laid a reassuring hand on Sister Hansen's shoulder and said soothingly, "Alright, I promise you I will take care of him, and now you must rest."

With Letta's calming answer, Sister Hansen's body tensed and then relaxed and at that moment on Easter Sunday, April 16, 1921, she slipped away into eternity to meet her God and her Creator.

The moment Letta realized that Sister Hansen had passed away, the full significance of her dying request burst forth into Letta's heart. Letta did not have many days to ponder or consider the request, as she herself soon fell ill with the deadly Typhus fever.

She lay for days burning with fever. Tossing and turning, Letta became delirious. A Norwegian missionary nurse came to nurse her back to health. Letta had drained her energy with caring for Sister Hansen, and now it seemed she had no strength to fight off the disease. The nurse struggled to keep her alive, but it appeared that the battle was soon to be lost. Letta finally breathed her last breath, and her nurse broke down in heart-wrenching sobs. She clung to Letta's lifeless body and bathed her with her tears.

Letta felt her spirit leave her body and glide slowly upwards. As she looked back down to where she had been lying on the bed, she saw the Norwegian nurse sitting next to the bed, crying over her lifeless body. Her spirit left the room, and then she could see a river; as she approached the river she noticed someone was with her. Somehow she knew that it was an angel. Instead of going through the river, they went over the river. She wondered at this, as she thought they would have to go into the river to get across.

Letta and the angel came upon throngs of people. In the midst of this multitude of people there shone a brilliant light. She could not look directly into the light. Letta realized that all these people were singing a song, which had the most beautiful melody. And though she had not heard the song before, she was thrilled by it and found herself joining in and singing along with the people.

Suddenly and without warning, the angel tapped her shoulder and told her that it was time to go back. Letta pulled back and said, "But I don't want to go back. I want to stay here."

The angel produced a rope and said, "This represents your life, and you have only lived this much." (As he measured it on the rope, it was only a small portion). "You have to go back and live the rest of the time. This is God's will for you."

Immediately they began their descent back into the room where she'd been lying ill; one moment she saw her body and then in the next she was back in her body.

She opened her eyes and saw her nurse still sitting there crying over her. When she realized that Letta was alive, she began to rejoice! Letta, still weak from her sickness, could manage a smile and nothing more. But her nurse's joy could not be contained, and she kept exclaiming at the miraculous thing that had taken place.

The nurse kept asking Letta over and over again, "What was that beautiful melody you were singing, and where did you learn it?"

Letta couldn't remember the tune or the words, but she felt sure it must have been what she had heard in heaven when she was in the very presence of God!

She had tasted the wonders of heaven, and now she knew that she could join with the apostle Paul in saying, "To live is Christ and to die is gain!" Whether she remained on earth to live out her life for Jesus or whether she went to be with Him in glory, she knew she would be happy! She no longer needed to fear sickness or what mankind could do to her, for her heavenly Father had graciously shown her His glory and His presence!

The others in the mission were overjoyed with Letta's recovery. They related to her how they had knelt in the small chapel of the mission and prayed, asking God to spare Letta's life. While they were praying, they heard Letta singing a beautiful melody, so they raced to the room to see her. They praised God when they saw the miracle that had taken place!

God continued strengthening Letta, and after a short time she was fully recovered.

Letta's heart remained saddened with the loss of dear Sister Hansen. She kept the promise that she had made to Sister Hansen tucked away deep in her heart. She was not sure how she would fulfill that promise. She didn't want to be distracted from the high calling the Lord had put on her life.

As soon as her body was strong enough, she returned to her daily routine. She worked diligently at the mission, preaching and doing visitations and making new personal contacts, all the while singing in her heart that she was allowed to do this for her Jesus.

She kept her promise to Sister Hansen by making sure that at all times Rev. Hansen was well taken care of. She saw to it that he took his meals regularly. She would often speak to the cook and encourage him to make things that she knew Rev. Hansen liked to eat. The days flew by, and before Letta knew it, she was celebrating her second Christmas in China. In the midst of her busy schedule, Letta hardly realized that something new had taken place. She could not begin to realize what had caused it, but one day Rev. Hansen looked upon her with a different look in his eye. He saw her through the eyes of love.

God had spoken to Rev. Hansen's heart that Letta would be his new life partner, his wife. He hesitated telling her, not knowing what she would think. He feared she would reject his idea, since there was a 16-year age difference between them. After much prayer, he could not hold himself back any longer. He approached Letta and carefully laid out his desire for the two of them to embark upon a friendship

"Sister Teuber, I would like you to pray about our entering a friendship together," Harold said.

Letta just stared at him, unsure of what her reply should be. Her head was spinning as she wondered how she would answer him. After some time, she gathered her thoughts and spoke up.

"Rev. Hansen, I assure you I will take this up in prayer. You can be sure that I will give this careful consideration."

Although no answer was given that day, Harold Hansen knew in his heart that Letta would diligently seek God for her direction. One of the main reasons he felt so drawn towards this young lady was her diligence in seeking God's face. She had a constant desire to do only what God wanted her to do, and that caused him to admire her.

Letta battled in her spirit as she prayed regarding Harold's request. God reminded her that as a teenager, He had spoken to her that she would marry a man named Hansen. She remembered how angry she had become. In her teenage mindset she'd stubbornly determined that she had no intention of marrying a "Hansen!"

Her first response to the Lord had been, "Why would I want to marry a man with such a common name?" There were many people she knew who bore the name Hansen.

But now, as she remembered what God had told her, she realized that marrying Harold Hansen would fulfill God's promise to her as well as the promise she'd made to Margaret Hansen in the final precious moments of that dear woman's life.. But still, she didn't come to this decision easily; she continually prayed for complete assurance.

During her time of prayer, she released the old feelings she sometimes still felt for her former boyfriend, Berthel. They had been so close that they were able to know what the other was thinking before even speaking. What a wonderful friendship had developed between them.

Although they were never officially engaged, everyone assumed they would be married. Sadly, one day Berthel fell ill and died. Letta's heart was crushed; she couldn't contain the sorrow that weighed her down. Letta recovered over the months that passed, but in her heart she carried the loss of her beloved Berthel. She knew that if she wanted to receive an answer from God regarding her future, she MUST release anything that stood in the way.

"Oh, Father, I give to you my all. Whatever you want for my life, oh Lord, that is what I want," Letta prayed earnestly.

In the stillness of the night, she felt God telling her that Rev. Hansen would be her husband. Peace flooded over her, and she knew her time of seeking had ended.

The next day, Letta rose up early and went to tell Rev. Hansen the decision she had made. He couldn't believe his ears. Trying to calm himself, he found his voice and asked her, "Letta, are you sure you want to make this decision? Are you sure you want to embark on this new course of life?"

"Oh, Rev. Hansen, the course of my life had already been ordered by the Lord. I just hadn't seen it clearly. But now the Lord has clearly shown me that this is definitely of Him."

She told Harold in detail of how the Lord had ordained her path and prepared her heart for this day to happen.

When Letta made the decision to travel to China for missions work, she had forever thrown off any thoughts of getting married. She gave herself totally to Jesus, having come to terms with the prospect of being single. But here God had chosen to abundantly bless her with this wonderful man. God's ways and workings would never cease to amaze her.

Harold and Letta chose to set their wedding date for June 2, 1922. What a celebration would surround this day, the day that their friendship would move into the closer intimacy of marriage.

Rev. Hansen was the chairman of the North China District Council for the Assemblies of God. All the missionaries knew him and loved him, so it was natural that everyone wanted to come and attend this glorious occasion. Missionaries were invited from everywhere to share in the blessed event. When they arrived in Peking, they were housed at the missionary compound. Oh, what a hustle and bustle there was!

The night before the wedding, a prayer meeting was held for those who had come to attend the wedding. The power of God fell over the meeting, and suddenly a single missionary woman rose and began to speak out, saying that the wedding should not be carried through. As she continued speaking, confusion enveloped the place.

Letta cried out to God, then and there, and asked Him to tell her what in the world was going on!

"Father, how can this be happening? What is this?"

"Child, do you not know my voice by now? Have you not prayed diligently for my answer in regards to your marriage?" God's voice brought peace to her heart.

"But Father, what of this woman's prophecy?" Letta pressed further.

No answer came, but peace enveloped her. This marriage was of God, and this "prophecy" had not been of God. Those in the assembly discussed and prayed together about what the woman had spoken. The other leaders judged the outburst and found it was not a prophetic word from God. The word had been given with ulterior motives. The final decision was that the wedding should go on as planned. All present recognized that this was a word of confusion that had not come from God.

The next morning Letta arose feeling nervous, as any bride would be. She gazed out the window, marveling at how the day looked more beautiful than any other day she had ever seen. The confusion and torment of the night before had no effect on her now. She turned and picked up her simple white frock, holding it close to herself.

"Oh, heavenly Father, could this really be happening to me? Am I really to

be wed on this day?" Letta's face shone with delight!

A touch of sadness fell as she remembered that her family couldn't be here to join in this celebration with her. How she longed for her brothers and sisters and her parents! But as quickly as the thought of home had entered her head, the Lord reminded her that those waiting outside were NEW brothers and sisters, in Christ, more than she had ever had before. They were going to join her on this wonderful day to witness her happiness.

Letta put her face forward to this new life she would now embark on. She knew there would be many things she had never encountered, but as always she knew that if Jesus was with her, then she would be all right.

Before she knew what was happening, there at her door were some of her missionary women friends, offering her their assistance. Someone handed her a beautiful rose bouquet with a satin ribbon tied around the middle. Someone else pushed her white pumps towards her and told her she should hurry and put them on. She smiled. Her quiet contemplation ended and the joyful mood of the day engulfed her!

Letta walked down the aisle to join herself with Harold Hansen, and in doing so she moved towards the new path God had laid out before her.

Letta and Harold Hansen on their wedding day

3

A fter the wedding, Letta moved into Rev. Hansen's residence at 9 Hsun Pu Ting Hutung in West City, Peking. They drew closer together both in their love for each other and in their love for the Lord Jesus Christ.

Letta continued with her street evangelism, ministering to anyone who needed help. Now as a married woman she had both her ministry and her husband to take care of. She must take time to get used to this new balancing act.

Rev. Hansen was still very involved in the prison ministry. He felt such a burden for those in the jails. Every week he went to the jails and to preach the gospel. People were amazed at this man's compassion for those whom society had given up on, but Letta encouraged him and gave him the support he needed to accomplish all that God had put in his heart to do.

Many people came to know Jesus as their personal savior and Lord through the street meetings and through the jail ministry. As the people would get saved, the Hansens led them into the next step of obedience to Christ, the step of water baptism. So often the unsaved family members of the converts would resist this step of obedience. Some of the converts were beaten with sticks and ropes in an attempt to prevent them from being baptized. In all this the Hansens would minister to the converts, building them up with the Word of God and supporting them with much prayer.

As the year progressed, Letta felt happier than she had ever felt before. She saw God at work in the ministry and in her home. The first months of marriage were filled with much joy despite any problems or difficulties that crossed their path.

The hot months were upon them, and yet they kept working diligently to accomplish all they had to do. Letta never rested; she was always busy helping others. Those who had problems or needs knew they could come to her and find her to be more than willing to help them in any way she could.

The days grew colder and shorter as winter approached. Letta couldn't keep up with her normal schedule; she often found herself needing to lie down for an afternoon nap or to just simply flop down into a chair for a quick rest. Harold had been used to seeing his new bride with so much energy that it worried him to see her looking so pale and tired.

"Letta, please rest, you know how easy it is to become sick." He said.

"Don't worry, I'm fine!"

"You mustn't take this lightly!" insisted Harold.

Letta glanced down at her hands and then, lifting her eyes, she looked at her husband with a smile playing at the corner of her mouth.

"It's ok; what is affecting me has affected many other women, and they have come through it just fine!"

Harold looked at his wife, confused.

"Do you know your sickness? But you haven't even seen a doctor yet, so how can you know what is wrong with you?"

"Dear, dear Harold, I am not sick! Don't you know?" Letta continued to tease him.

"Letta, tell me what you are talking about! I am too old for this cat and mouse game you are playing," Harold commanded.

"We are going to have a child!" Letta exclaimed. Harold was speechless! He stared at his beautiful wife who seemed all the more lovely at this moment.

He tried to respond but the words failed him. He just stared at his amazing wife.

Letta and Harold with other mission workers

"Harold, are you ok?" Letta asked. "Letta...Letta...I am at a loss for words at this moment! When did you find out, and when will the baby come? I have so many questions. I want you to rest. You must cut down your workload."

Advice tumbled out of Harold's mouth. Letta blushed at her husband's concern. She was so used to being the one who took care of others, it was difficult for her to know how to handle all this attention.

"Harold, I'm fine. God knows all things, and nothing is done without His knowledge, so I have a deep assurance that all will be well! And now I look forward to this baby. What joy I feel!"

Harold strode across the room to where Letta was standing and embraced her. She seemed so slight, almost like a child in his arms, how amazing that she would be embarking on this path of motherhood. But as with all the new roads in her life, Letta journeyed the road of motherhood with determination and strength that only God could give.

Much to Harold's dismay, his wife didn't lighten her schedule. She became busier than ever, going about the city doing whatever needed to be done. Together they kept busy doing street witnessing and visiting the jails. Being the pastor's wife, Letta had the responsibility of taking care of the women in the church. During her daily visitations, members of the church would introduce her to their neighbors who wanted prayer.

Letta visited those who were in need and prayed for them, even taking care of them as they lay sick in bed. Somehow she always seemed to know those who didn't have enough to eat and she would bring along some extra food to share with them. Her love shone to all those she came in contact with.

It thrilled Letta's heart each time she taught people from the Bible. She could see their eyes brighten as they heard the Good News of what Jesus Christ did for them. After she would share with them from the Word of God, she spent time praying for people she had talked to. With excitement she would face each new day, knowing that each day gave her the opportunity to share the wonderful love of Jesus.

One day, she awoke early and began to pray for the day ahead. She prayed for a while in English and then found herself praying in tongues. After praying for some time, Letta stopped abruptly. She was troubled and decided to ask God about something that was bothering her.

She spoke to God, saying, "Father, I'm sorry, but I need to know something. Why do I need to speak in this prayer language? What is the purpose of it all?" When she asked the question, God dropped a couple of verses into her heart. She knew them all too well:

"And in the same way the Spirit also helps our weaknesses; for we do not know how to pray as we should but the Spirit Himself intercedes for us with groaning too deep for words; and He who searches the hearts knows what the mind of the Spirit is, because He intercedes for the saints according to the will of God" (Romans 8:26 and 27).

"But Lord, I know those verses! Why can't the Spirit pray through me in English! What is the purpose of praying in this language that I can't understand?" Letta persisted.

The heavens seemed silent, so Letta continued once again to allow the tongues to flow from her innermost being, but then she stopped abruptly when she realized suddenly that she was hearing English words pouring forth, yet she was not controlling her words or thinking of what to say. The English words just flowed out of her, and she began to listen to what she was saying.

Her voice rose in intercession, "Have mercy on Mrs. Wong. She needs strength to overcome her opium habit!"

Letta clamped her hand tightly over her mouth as soon as she heard what she had said. She shook her head in disbelief.

"Oh, Father, how could I have said that?! Mrs. Wong is one of our main members in the church; she doesn't have an opium habit."

Distraught, Letta continued to pray. For awhile she prayed with her mind, controlling every word that came out of her mouth, but then she felt herself praying once again in the Spirit. The words that tumbled out of her mouth were in clear English! Amazed, Letta listened to what she her spirit said, and once again the prayer was for Mrs. Wong's supposed opium habit.

Jumping to her feet, Letta said aloud, "I will settle this once and for all! I will go to Mrs. Wong's house right now and get to the bottom of this!"

Picking up her coat and throwing it over her shoulders, she strode out of the house. All the way down the street she struggled within herself to grasp what had just happened! She reached Mrs. Wong's house and entered through the main gate. A servant girl ran forward greeting her warmly, "Oh, Sister Hansen, welcome, welcome! Please come inside."

"I need to see Mrs. Wong, please, it is urgent!" Letta said.

"One moment, you sit down please, Sister Hansen, I will go and see if she is resting."

The maid led Letta to a chair facing the doorway of Mrs. Wong's bedroom.

As Letta sat stiffly on the straight-backed chair, she wondered what she would say when Mrs. Wong came out to see her. Her mind argued with her at the foolishness of her visit. Within a few minutes, the young girl returned with a nervous expression on her face.

"I'm sorry, but Mrs. Wong is resting now. I think it is best that I do not disturb her at this time." The girl fidgeted as she spoke.

Letta tried to gather her thoughts; she waited for a couple of seconds, and then she replied, "I will wait."

"Oh, no, you must not wait, she will take some time to rest!" blurted out the maid, now appearing extremely agitated.

"No, I will wait, even if it takes all day." Letta settled herself against the hard back of the chair and adjusted her dress.

The servant girl stared in astonishment, not knowing what to do with Letta's response. She moved from one foot to the other, and then darted back into the bedroom. The door opened, but this time the girl didn't come out of the room; instead it was Mrs. Wong herself who emerged. She stopped short when she saw Letta sitting in front of her.

Mrs. Wong stretched her arms out in front of her and stumbled forward, crying as she ran, "Oh, Sister Hansen! Oh, you have found me out! You have found me out!"

She fell into Letta's arms. Letta held her close, patting her back, unsure of what was going on. She tried to quiet Mrs. Wong, but she continued to cry uncontrollably.

"What is it Mrs. Wong? What is the matter? Why are you crying so?" Letta asked, gently.

Between heart-wrenching sobs, Mrs. Wong said, "Sister Hansen, you have found out about my smoking opium! I... it is so bad... how did you know? I have kept this a secret, but today... you came just as I was in my room... preparing to smoke the opium! Now you know! Oh, what will you think of me?"

Letta continued to hug her, amazed by what she had heard. She began to pray for her. She held no condemning thoughts; all she could think of was the amazing mercy of their heavenly Father!

"My dear sister, do not feel ashamed, for God loves you! He sent me here not to condemn you, but to pray with you and to help you free yourself from this habit!" Letta whispered to the sobbing woman.

With the prayer and the kind words, Letta could feel the tension in Mrs. Wong's body ebbing away. Her sobs turned into cleansing tears, and a sweet spirit enveloped her. Slowly she lifted her head and looked up into Letta's face.

"Thank you! Oh, thank you, Sister Hansen, for you have shown me love and forgiveness. I know that I am set free from this wicked habit that has been holding me captive for years! I feel somehow different within myself. Oh, thank you, and thank God for His kindness in sending you here to me!"

After the prayer was over, she gathered her things and said her necessary good-byes. She journeyed back down the street towards her own home, in awe at the magnificent knowledge of God!

"Oh, Father in Heaven, You know all things! You are able to see ALL things, even those done in secret! And now I understand that when I pray in tongues, my spirit is praying and interceding for the saints. Father, the secrets that are shared in the prayer language are too much for me to bear; please Lord, I don't mind praying in tongues anymore! I realize now that it is important and nothing to be taken lightly. Forgive me for doubting You or questioning Your ways, for Your ways are higher than mine, and Your thoughts are not my thoughts. In Jesus' name, amen."

As she finished praying, Letta rounded the corner and entered her own compound. She felt somehow lighter, knowing that God understood her questioning and had such mercy to show her His reason for allowing her to speak in tongues. Now she knew speaking in tongues was indeed a privilege, not some- thing to be taken lightly. She rushed into the house, anxious to share this testimony with her husband.

The months sped by, and before Letta knew it, the time had arrived for her to deliver her baby. In the wee hours of the morning of August 13, 1923, Letta woke up to the feeling of pain. She realized that these pains were the pains of childbirth, so she quickly woke Harold and asked him to call the doctor.

Dr. Sun was asked to come to the house. Before Dr. Sun arrived, the house filled up with the hustle and bustle of those preparing for the new arrival. As soon as the doctor arrived, he took over.

By 3 p.m. that afternoon, little Viola Letta Hansen lay snuggled in Letta's arms. Harold stood by his wife's bedside and gazed at his two precious girls. Letta couldn't seem to take her eyes off her little bundle of joy. She looked up at Harold and smiled.

"Oh, Harold, she is ours!" Letta exclaimed.

Harold could only nod smilingly, as he felt himself overcome with joy. He placed his hand on Letta's shoulder and patted her. He was amazed that at the age of 41 this was the first child to bless his home. He was indeed a proud and happy father.

"Now, you must rest, dear!" He said.

Letta looked up at him in surprise, "Rest? But I want to enjoy this new baby of mine. I can't seem to look at her enough. I thank God for giving me such a lovely little baby."

As Letta looked back down at her baby, Viola, she felt as though she was back on that ship deck, looking out on her new "home" country. Here she was once again, looking out towards her new horizons, her new destinations in life, and what joy flooded her. She didn't know what was ahead, but she knew that God would go before her and direct her in all the things she needed to accomplish for His name's sake.

4

L ife never had a dull moment. With ministry responsibilities and her new baby, Letta was kept busy throughout the day. Harold felt God putting a strong desire in his heart to start a Bible school in the city. Many of the converts needed to know more about walking with Jesus, and he knew that a local Bible school would help them grow in their spiritual lives. Both Letta and Rev. Hansen had a strong desire to see local leaders raised up to take care of the churches across China. Letta prayed with her husband over the plans of starting a Bible school. They were excited to see what God had in store for them in this new venture.

Harold managed to acquire a large building in which to hold the classes. He named this new school the Truth Bible Institute. Several of the missionaries joined with Rev. Hansen to teach in the school. Letta found that she had been chosen to teach some of the classes, and so this was yet another task added to her already hectic schedule. Her heart thrilled as she studied the Word in preparation and then got up in front of the students to expound on what she had studied.

The Word of God shared at the Bible school went forth with life and power. Lives began to change, and the students grew in the Lord. Many of the students were former prisoners who were saved under Rev. Hansen's jail ministry. Now they sat and soaked in the Good News, and they found their lives being transformed even more. These students burned with a

Letta and 5-month-old Viola

strong desire to go forth into their nation and see many come to know the true knowledge of Jesus Christ and all that He had done for them!

At 4:30 each morning, Letta slipped out of bed and went into her little office area. Sitting with her Bible on her lap, she enjoyed the sweet presence of God as she allowed His Spirit to minister to her. Nothing in the world could compare to these times she spent alone with her precious Friend and Savior. Every day she thanked Him for what He was doing in her life; never could she have imagined that He would bless her the way He had. God had allowed her to be instrumental in ministering to many people. She felt it was such a privilege to be part of what God was doing in China, and she rejoiced as she witnessed lives changing right before her eyes. God had blessed her with a wonderful husband and a beautiful baby girl, and life couldn't get any sweeter.

With the dawning of the New Year, 1924, Viola grew cuter by the day. Sweet warmth seeped into Letta's heart every time she watched Harold sing little Viola to sleep. She looked so tiny, snuggled in her husband's muscular arms. When she wasn't sleeping she was busy crawling around the house.

Whenever she had a spare moment, Letta would throw a fur rug on the floor and watched contentedly as her baby kicked and played. Every gurgle or smile from her darling daughter brought such joy to Letta's heart.

Not only did Letta's heart thrill with her baby's progress, but she also found herself thrilled at the progress of the "babes in Christ" with whom she had contact. They grew in leaps and bounds in the Lord, moving forward rapidly in the ways of God.

During the year of 1924, Harold and Letta stepped up their street evangelism. They would travel to nearby villages with two or three of their Bible school students, and once in the village, they would stand in the marketplace and share the Good News of Jesus to all who were near. People were hungry for good news. The year had been filled with various problems; war, flood, and famine had attempted to steal their hope. As the Hansens shared the Word of God, hope sprang up in hearts and many came to know the Lord. Hearts and lives were transformed.

With the growth in the work, Rev. Hansen began to contemplate the construction of a new church building. The building they currently used was simply not large enough to accommodate all the people.

Every new project started by her husband caused Letta to be more involved in activities. Time flew by, and before Letta realized it, October had arrived. Viola was no longer just crawling; she had learned to pull herself up on every available piece of furniture she could find. On October 20th, Viola let go of all secure furnishings and took her first step. Letta couldn't believe her baby was walking, and in her joy she scooped up her daughter in her arms, swung her around, And announced happily,

"My sweet baby, you have taken the biggest step of your life! For now you will be able to walk and run and explore as never before!" Viola wriggled in her mother's arms as she showered her with loving kisses.

"Life can't get any better than this!" Thought Letta as she allowed her daughter to wriggle out   of her arms and watched her toddle off to explore the rest of the house under the watchful eye of her nanny.

Letta returned to working on the lesson plans for her Bible School class. Towards afternoon, a soft knock on the door interrupted her study. She glanced up to see Viola's nanny standing there speechless, looking distraught.

"Please come in!" Letta urged, but not waiting to find out what was wrong, she ran towards Viola's room. Her daughter lay in her bed burning with fever. Within just a short time she had thrown up several times causing her body to become weak. Letta attempted to get some liquids down her throat, but nothing would stay down. Picking her baby up, she paced the floor with her and prayed over her.

"Please go and find Rev. Hansen," Letta pleaded to the nanny.

While she waited for her husband to arrive, she tried everything she could think of to relieve Viola of her suffering, but nothing seemed to help. It seemed like an eternity before her husband burst through the doors of the bedroom.

"Harold, Viola is so sick! I'm scared! Please call a doctor. Tell Dr. Sun to come immediately and take a look at dear Viola."

Never had Letta felt as helpless as she felt at that moment. Her heart broke as she watched her darling daughter suffering.

Dr. Sun was summoned, and after examining Viola, he determined she had dysentery. He encouraged the Hansens to give her plenty of liquids. He gave them some medications that he said might help to stop the baby from vomiting, but he couldn't offer much assistance. As Letta looked at her husband and back at their little girl, she prayed silently to keep her mind free of the anxiety that lurked within her, trying to take control. She knelt down next to her daughter's crib and stroked her tiny arm, praying silently.

Feeling too restless to remain still, Letta stood up and began to pace the floor. Each step she took was an attempt to flee the disturbance in her spirit, but no matter how much she paced she couldn't escape from it. Exhaustion engulfed her like a heavy cloud. Through the heaviness, she heard the familiar voice of her Master, "Come unto me, all ye that labor and are heavy laden, and I will give you rest."

Letta dropped to her knees, sobbing, "Oh, my Jesus! Why was I trying to escape this turmoil on my own? I should have been running to You. Forgive me for trying to bear this burden alone, Oh Lord — I need you to bear this for me."

Peace came down and dispelled the heaviness that had surrounded her. She rose from her knees and went to lie down.

Despite how tired she was, Letta could not sleep. She got back up and hovered over Viola throughout the night. At 12.30am, little Viola's body sagged into the bed. Her eyelids fluttered and a gentle moan escaped her rosebud lips. Letta started forward, leaning over to see if Viola wanted some water. She could hear her daughter gasping for air, and she watched, helplessly, as the life slipped out of Viola's tiny body.

At 12.45am., on the chilly morning of October 21, 1924, Letta held the body of her lifeless daughter tightly in her arms and wept with overpowering sorrow as she had never experienced it before, sweeping over her in massive waves. She began to moan and sob as searing emotional pain raced through every part of her being.

Her heart-wrenching sobs awakened her husband from sleep; he bolted out of the bed and ran to her side. Seeing Viola's limp body in Letta's arms, Harold understood what had happened, and he began to weep bitterly. He wrapped his arms around his wife and pulled her to himself, attempting to shield her from this pain she now had to bear.

Letta's distraught sobs could only be verbalized with one agonizing word that poured from her repeatedly as she cried, "Why? Why?"

Harold had no answer to his wife's question.

He just held her tighter. Letta continued to weep helplessly over the loss of her darling baby. Harold strode out of the room to get the doctor, hoping there would be some way to bring his daughter back to life. When he returned with the doctor, they slowly pried Viola from Letta's arms and gently laid her body in her crib. After the doctor examined her, he verified that nothing more could be done for little Viola Letta Hansen.

Gently Harold drew Letta up and helped her to the bed, encouraging her to lie down. Letta just sat stiffly at the edge of the bed, crying uncontrollably.

Shaking her head from side to side, she kept asking, "Why? Why?"

She knew there was no answer and yet she felt she had to keep asking. Her mind tried to make sense of this. Hadn't she been so happy just a short while earlier? Hadn't everything seemed to be so perfect? How could things change so drastically in such a short time?

At last, too exhausted to cry, she fell back onro her bed and lay staring blankly up at the bed frame.

Harold left the room with the doctor, and now Letta felt so very alone. The emptiness was almost unbearable.

"I need You now, Jesus, my lover and my friend; I need You now more than ever! I cannot understand this loss; I have no answer to the question "why"... please, Jesus, please come and take me in Your arms. I need Your comfort and Your strength to be able to go on. I fear that I cannot go on in my own strength! This is too much for my heart of bear."

As always, God answered her quickly, allowing His peace to descend upon her. She felt the blanket of His Love covering her, and found hcr eyes closing to rest as she snuggled into His comforting arms. She found comfort under His wings and she found rest in Him.

The early morning light playfully flickered across Letta's face causing her to waken from her sound sleep. She rubbed her sleepy eyes with the back of her hand as she yawned. Rolling over on her side, she forced her heavy eyelids to open. Drowsily she surveyed the room, wondering if what she had experienced the previous night could have been a nightmare.

Icy thoughts of reality pierced through her stupor as she jumped up and stumbled to the crib only to find it empty! The emptiness of the crib reminded her of the empty feeling she felt inside her heart. Clinging to the side of the crib, a groan escaped Letta's lips. Her knees buckled under her and, falling onto the floor, she cried out to God for strength to go through this horrible darkness.

Sorrow filled the days ahead, leaving Harold and Letta emotionally exhausted. The other missionaries and the Chinese Christians rallied around the Hansens, giving them encouragement and support in their time of mourning. Letta could feel the love of the saints

engulfing her, and even though it brought a sense of comfort to her, she still could not deny a hollow emptiness that lingered deep within.

On the day of the funeral, Letta stood stoically next to Harold at the British cemetery in Peking. They both watched the small casket slowly disappearing down into the cold, gaping hole. As the casket was being lowered into the ground, Letta buried an equally heavy burden of pain and hurt and confusion into the deep recesses of her innermost being. God desired to lift that burden from her immediately, but this was one burden that Letta seemed unable to release as easily as others. The pain and horror of losing her baby daughter were too great to comprehend, so instead she closed the door on those raw feelings and forged ahead with her usual brave stoicism.

So, turning away from the gravesite, Letta put her face towards the future, determining that she would not allow this loss to cause her to stumble or to get in the way of what needed to be done in the land God had called her to.

Although Letta's heart was determined, the months ahead proved to be difficult. When she would return from her teaching or her times of ministry, the silence in the house overpowered her. She longed to hear the familiar sound of Viola's gurgling laughter which once greeted her so joyfully. Her arms ached with the need to embrace that soft little body which had so readily snuggled into her bosom. Each time the unbearable longings rose up within her, Letta would run desperately to the feet of Jesus. It was only at the feet of the Master where she found comfort and solace from the deep loss.

God continually upheld Letta. She felt His strength flow through her being, enabling her to continue with His work. The joy of serving Him strengthened her as she never thought she could be strengthened.

One cold morning, Letta crept out of bed to have her usual quiet time with God. How she treasured the times she sat at His feet and felt His continual refreshing. She opened her Bible and began to read a passage of scripture, delighting at the way the Holy Spirit opened her eyes to the truths hidden in each line. Sliding the Bible across the floor in front of her, Letta stretched herself out on the floor. She meditated on what the Word had said and she felt challenged once again to keep preaching the Good News so that she could see the captives be set free.

A loud knock on the front door interrupted her time of meditation. Letta scrambled to her feet and waited to hear from the doorkeeper who could be visiting at this early hour.

Before long she heard the shuffling of the door-keeper's feet as he made his way down the hall. He entered the room and informed her that there was a desperate woman pleading to see her. The woman at the gate stood tall and proud, but her clothing told a tale of hard times. As Letta approached the woman she dropped to her knees at Letta's feet and began sobbing.

"Please, get up!" Letta urged the woman.

The woman refused to rise. She held on to Letta's feet, weeping all the more. Letta slid down next to her and put her arms around her.

"Please, tell me what is wrong," Letta, said.

Letta now realized that the woman was much younger than she had first assumed. Her sobs subsided and she began to pour out her tragic story. She had no money to pay a debt she owed. Her daughter, who had been put in an orphanage nearby, would be used to repay the debt she owed. The tragedy was that if she could not repay her debt, then she would lose her daughter forever. The thought of her daughter being used as a bargaining chip for her debt broke her heart and she couldn't contain her sobs another moment.

"Oh, please Mrs. Hansen, I have heard of you. I know you are a good woman. You have helped many people. Please help my daughter!" The words tumbled out, running together like unruly dogs chasing each other down a hill.

Viola's funeral

Letta sat back, trying to absorb what she had heard. She felt the mother's heart breaking at the thought of losing her daughter. She knew that young girls were taken to orphanages because the parents couldn't afford to take care of them. But even in those places there was always a chance for the children to be reunited with their parents. But if this young girl was handed over to repay the debt owed, there would be no chance for the mother and daughter to be reunited. The seven-year-old child would be forced to enter a life of misery. The memory of the pain of her own loss gripped her heart. She had not been able to stop Viola's little spirit from slipping away from her, but now she could do something to help this woman not lose her daughter.

"Please wait here," Letta told the woman, before she dashed away.

It didn't take her long to present the need to her husband. He immediately saw the dire situation and realized that something had to be done fast. They discussed their course of action and then went back to the lady to inform her of their plan to help her redeem her daughter.

Together the Hansens went with the woman to pay the debt that was owed. A feeling of relief overcame them once the debt was cleared. The woman's face glowed and she couldn't stop thanking them for their kindness.

"Come with me," she begged the Hansens.

They looked at each other curiously. Where did she want to take them? At first they protested, as they had to get back to their normal daily schedules. The woman pleaded with them all the more.

"Please, I want you to come with me to where my daughter is. I want you to meet her," she explained.

It didn't take long for them to make their way across town to the orphanage. As they drew near to the rambling old house, they saw many little girls strolling about. One little girl ran towards them shouting, "Mama!"

The Hansens soon realized the mother's intentions. She had brought them to meet her daughter in hopes that they would take her from the orphanage and make her their own child. No matter how much they refused, Letta found that the mother continued to plead with them. Finally the Hansens agreed to go home and pray over this unusual request. Letta already knew that this bright young Chinese girl had captured her heart.

After much prayer and contemplation, they agreed to take in this beautiful little girl and raise her as their own daughter. Together they went to the orphanage to bring their new daughter home. Lois was now part of the Hansen family. Instead of the former gloomy silence, laughter now filled their home once again.

The year 1925 brought even more joy and laughter, as Letta discovered that she was pregnant again. She was amazed by God's mercy. The Hansens were amazed at how God was continuing to bless them; they both joined together to look forward to the arrival of their new blessing. Once more they expectantly turned their faces from what was past and looked to that which was ahead.

5

The New Year came with much hustle and bustle. The Hansens were very involved with working on a new building. They had already opened a new mission on a busy Chinese street. All their outreach ministries were growing and bursting at the seams. Truly God was doing marvelous things for them.

Rev. Hansen found himself frustrated with supervising the building project. He would want something done one way, and invariably it would be done a completely different way. Daily he had to pray for patience. Often he would overhear the workers telling each other in Chinese, "These foreign devils are too picky." He didn't know whether to laugh or to be upset by these remarks.

Not only did the Hansens have to face the pressures of their work, but they also faced political upheaval and unrest. The Nationalist movement was gaining momentum. The northern warlords were fighting battles. Student movements were determined to stir up antagonism towards the missionaries and their mission schools. In the midst of all this turmoil, Harold fell ill. At first Letta thought it might just be over-exhaustion due to the strain he had been under during the past few months.

"Don't get out of bed today!" Letta commanded Harold. "It may be nothing, but still you need your rest. You have told me yourself that we can never be too careful."

Harold ignored his wife's advice and tried to get out of the bed anyway, but exhaustion overcame him.

"Letta, I'm sorry, but I do think I will need to rest! Can you take over the duties for today?" Harold mumbled weakly.

"Of course I don't mind. The important thing is for you to rest and get better," she assured her husband as she tucked the blankets around him.

Letta rushed off to the Bible school, leaving instructions for someone to keep an eye on her husband. Unfortunately, his condition continued to deteriorate as the day progressed. Toward evening, Letta dashed into the house and immediately went in to check on her husband. To her utter dismay she discovered that he had vomited blood. Taking a deep breath, Letta endeavored to release the pressure that was seeking to constrict her chest. She knew that this was no time to panic; she had to think clearly and take care of her husband.

"I'm going to call the doctor." Letta said, almost to herself.

Harold protested weakly, "Letta...I just need a couple of days rest. I know I will get better."

Frowning, Letta touched his forehead. He didn't feel hot and he did look like he would improve with rest.

"Alright, I won't call the doctor today, but Harold, if you continue to get worse, I **will** get a doctor."

His condition did not improve, and much to Letta's dismay some pustules began to appear on his skin. Letta knew she had no choice but to call a doctor. The doctor arrived without delay and exam- ined her husband thoroughly. He frowned as he turned towards his medical bag, carefully putting his equipment away.

"Mrs. Hansen, I'm sorry to have to inform you that your husband has smallpox."

"Please tell me what we can do for him," begged Letta, still not realizing the full impact of what the doctor had just told her.

The doctor looked down at his bag and then back at Letta and replied, "My dear woman, I wish I could offer you some hopeful advice. Unfortunately there is no hope for your husband. There is nothing that can be done for him now. You can only try to keep him comfortable."

She stared defiantly at the doctor and then, pulling herself up, she faced him with fire in her eyes.

"Sir, I believe in prayer! And I know that my God has healed in the past and He will heal again!"

The doctor shook his head sadly as he picked up his bag to leave. He was sure that would be the last he saw of Rev. Hansen alive. Letta refused to allow what the doctor had said to sway her conviction that her husband would get up from his sick bed and be well again.

The next few days and weeks of Letta's life were completely engrossed in nursing her husband as best she could. At first Harold could respond to her questions, and he would actually try and comfort her.

"Shush, be quiet Harold, you need your energy. Don't worry about me. God is here and He will take care of you and me," Letta softly reassured her husband.

The fever and the red pustules covering his body turned his face beet red. Daily the pustules increased in number until they had spread out over every imaginable part of his body. The slightest amount of pressure caused the pustules to burst and ooze with pus. Letta became terrified to touch him in case she caused him more pain than he was already in.

Along with the pustules that now covered his entire body, Harold began to swell up terribly as well. His appearance had deteriorated to the point that he no longer even looked like a human being.

The neighbors demanded that they vacate the house due to the highly contagious nature of smallpox, but Letta didn't know where she could go with her husband in this condition. She had been keeping the room dark to protect Harold's eyes, as his eyes also had pustules in them.

Any clothing put on him became like sticky tape that pulled his skin right off when it was removed. Excruciating pain accompanied any movement or change of bedding. With all these considerations, Letta couldn't think of any place where Harold could be taken and still be cared for properly.

Soon the neighbors came to her and said, "We have found a place for you to take your husband. We will help you to leave here today." "Where would that be?" Letta wondered.

They replied, "It is an abandoned temple way up on the hillside outside the city."

Letta shuddered at the thought of it, but she knew she had no choice but to do as they said. She left the people waiting in the courtyard while she went inside to gather blankets and other necessary parcels to take along with her. After a short time of organizing people to help her carry Harold, she was ready to leave.

Walking up the side of the hill, Letta looked up to see the temple looming up ahead. She pulled her coat tighter and shivered. She wanted to turn around and dash back down the hill, and yet she knew she had no choice in this matter.

Arriving at the temple, Letta marched in and quickly put together some bedding on the floor. The men moved to put Harold down on the makeshift bed on the floor. Every movement the men made drew a sharp cry of pain. Letta darted forward reaching out, trying to gently ease his body down and adjust the bedclothes. Once he had been settled, the people bid Letta good-bye. After they left she closed the large wooden doors of the temple. With all her strength, she pulled down the heavy wooden bar that would bolt the door shut.

Turning around, Letta viewed the vast hall. All she had was a candle to light this large expanse, and in the flickering light of the candle she saw huge idols staring down upon them. The shadows of the figures played eerily on the walls.

"Oh, Father in heaven, how have I found myself in this place?" She whispered.

She lighted her way over to where her husband was lying on the floor. Her growing belly made it awkward for her to bend over. She stood over her husband and wondered how she would keep going on.

Desperate loneliness descended upon her. Her weary body bent under the pressure of feeling so VERY alone! She looked back down at Harold, hoping for some comfort, but he remained delirious, completely unaware of what she was facing at that moment.

Falling on her knees, Letta lifted her face to heaven and cried out, "Oh, Father, if ever I needed You, I need You now! Please strengthen me and be with me. You promised NEVER to leave me or to forsake me; I stand on that promise now. In Jesus' precious name, amen."

No sooner had the prayer escaped her lips than the warmth and presence of the living God surrounded her. She felt strength surging through her innermost being. She was able to find a comfortable position from which she could take care of her husband. Her main concern was to keep him comfortable.

Her eyes traveled lovingly across her husband's strained face. It was incredible that he was still surviving. In the two weeks since his sickness had started, he had come close to death many times.

Letta had painstakingly rubbed him down with oil to soothe his skin, and she used a little carbolic acid to try and stop the extreme itching. Nothing worked for long; the pain continued to be unbearable and the stench of the disease permeated every space. At least he was alive, and Letta knew that Harold must pull through! She would not allow herself to think of the thousands of people in China who had already died from this dreadful disease.

As Letta leaned over Harold, whispering to him that things would be all right, she heard the sound of the wind. A storm had risen, and the howling of the wind made this abandoned temple seem all the more desolate.

Letta attempted to rest, but the raging storm kept her awake. After some time she found herself dozing off, only to be awakened by a loud knocking on the huge wooden doors of the temple. Sitting up, she listened, and once again she heard the loud knocking. Letta clambered up and stumbled towards the doors, for she thought this was possibly some poor soul who had gotten lost in the terrible storm and now they were seeking shelter. As her hand touched the door, she heard the Lord say, "NO!"

She fell back in surprise. She tried to argue with the Lord.

Once again the knocking came and Letta instinctively moved forward to answer the door, but again she heard the Lord command, "No!"

"But God, how can you tell me not to open the door?" Letta questioned. "There may be someone out there who needs shelter from the storm, and I am being cruel to not try and help the person."

Even as she finished saying that, the knocking continued more persistently. She knew she must open the door so she moved forward again, but this time the Lord said firmly, "NO! Don't open the door!"

This time she KNEW she had to obey the Lord's voice. She moved back to her bedding, sat down slowly, and stared at the door.

Why, God, wouldn't you want me to open the door? I don't understand why, but I know that I must obey you, Letta prayed in her heart.

Letta felt her heart torn with the desire to obey her God and to help whoever was on the other side of the door. Her natural mind cried out for her to leap to her feet and open the door, but the Holy Spirit within her commanded her to stay where she was!

After much time, the knocking stopped. Letta couldn't help but wonder what she would find when she opened the door the next morning. She dreaded the thought and tried to force herself to fall asleep, but to no avail.

Early the next morning, she heard voices outside the door.

"Letta, are you okay?"

When she opened the huge doors, there were a group of missionaries anxiously wanting to know how she was. The missionaries told her that a large leopard had been prowling around. The villagers had seen him going towards the temple, but they'd had

no way to warn Letta. The missionaries had prayed that nothing would happen to her and that she would be kept safe.

When the missionaries inspected the door, they saw claw marks on it, and they also saw huge paw prints leading right up to the door. Letta continued to look at these things, suddenly realizing that the knocking sound had probably been from the tail of the leopard or from his clawing at the door! If she hadn't obeyed the voice of God the night before, she would have been mauled to death by the leopard.

When she related the incident to the missionaries, they just stood astounded at what God had done. Together they lifted up their voices in a prayer of thanksgiving to the Lord for His protection!

The missionaries urged her to return to the mission compound. They told her that they would help her in caring for her husband. Letta, exhausted beyond words, was thrilled with the offer of support.

Even more missionaries came to pray over Rev. Hansen, and the prayers offered in faith brought divine healing to his body. Over the next few days his condition improved. The pustules dried up. Harold regained consciousness and began to feel strength coming back into his body. No one could believe that Rev. Hansen had survived. Letta knew it was just one more proof that her God was a prayer-answering God.

Once Rev. Hansen was well enough, he sat down and wrote a letter of thanks to those faithful prayer warriors in the United States:

I have gone through the valley, and cold Jordan nearly enveloped me, but thanks be to God, who always causeth us to triumph through Christ, He has snatched me from the lion's mouth and today, after 26 days of suffering, I am able to pen these few lines.

Two brothers prayed for me at my bedside and the Weidman sisters, filled with the power of God, boldly came to my bedside and laid hands on me and prayed. At first the room seemed filled with demons, and while they prayed I saw hideous snakes between them and me, and little demon imps laughing and mocking. But, after steady holding on in faith, the Lord drove them out and the Shekinah glory filled the room, and the victory was the Lord's. That night I slept like a babe. For several nights the fever had been burning me up and all these nights I had no sleep. The next morning, the mantle fell on me and such a spirit of prayer to come on a sick body is indescribable. Ever since then heaven has come down and new faith in God has filled my heart.

Beloved, all things work together for good to them that love the Lord. In a word, Satan has been bruised, lost the fight and Jesus as ever is the Captain of my salvation. This poor man has again been spared to carry the glad news of the Gospel to the Chinese whom I love. Amen! Another week will see me free of the scabs. Will not write more now as I am weak.

Amazingly, Rev. Hansen experienced a speedy recovery. Before long he was up and around and he jumped right back into his busy schedule.

Letta also got back into her normal routine, but found she slowed down as the time drew closer for delivery. The days filled up with helping those at the mission, teaching Bible school classes, and doing visitations.

The day for Letta to deliver arrived. Both Letta and Harold rejoiced together on August 26, 1925, when little baby Gwendolyn Hazel Hansen was born. Letta couldn't contain her joy as she held her new daughter in her arms. She had been aching for a baby, and now God had given her another beautiful baby girl.

All around her people were distraught with all the civil upheaval that continued to plague the nation of China. The civil war had ravished the villages and families. But for Harold and Letta, the civil unrest that surrounded them didn't seem to matter at this point. With Gwendolyn snuggled in Letta's arms, the painful suffering of the past few months disappeared.

God took the Hansens safely through another winter in China. Wars and rumors of wars continued to plague them. Several thousands of wounded were brought to Peking for treatment. Despite all the negative things going on around them, they were moving forward doing what God wanted them to do. People's lives were continuing to be changed. The new building was officially opened.

By the time the new facility was dedicated, Letta had been in China for almost six years, and she and Harold decided they needed a rest, especially after the past year, which had been very stressful with sickness and civil unrest and the building project. The Hansens received permission to take a furlough.

Letta was overjoyed with the thought of going home to see her family. Gwendolyn was now almost six months old, and she couldn't wait for her family to see her daughter. So much had happened to her in the time since she had left her family. There had been so many changes. But in all things God had proved Himself to be her strength and her shield. He was her ever-present fortress in times of trouble.

Some Christians in Hawaii had sent some money for their fares, requesting that they stop over for a short time to rest there. Letta was thrilled. Although she was anxious to get home to see her family, she knew she and her husband would benefit from a short rest in Hawaii. She thanked God for His faithfulness in making such a wonderful provision for them. What a wonderful God to not only care for all their needs, but to give them their heart's desire as well.

6

After spending two years on furlough in the U.S., Letta and Harold set sail for China once again on February 4, 1928. So much had happened in the eight years since Letta took her first ship to China. She had been a single missionary at that time, and now she was a married woman with a beautiful daughter and pregnant with another child.

Letta had lived a lifetime in the past few years. She had battled with death in her own life and in the lives of the ones she loved. The loss of her firstborn child left a mark deep within her soul. Despite the trials and tribulations she went through, Letta knew that God had strengthened her.

The Hansens didn't know what sort of changes to expect when they reached China. They'd heard reports of continual fighting going on between the warlords. Chiang Kai-Shek and his nationalist army had moved forward capturing many cities. Despite the reports, Letta didn't feel afraid, for she knew that God would go before her family.

The journey back to China went smoothly. Letta thought she might deliver her baby on the ship, so she kept an American flag nearby to wrap the baby in if it was born onboard. Once the baby was wrapped in the flag, they would proclaim the baby a U.S. citizen. As it turned out, the Hansens arrived in China with the baby still growing safely inside her.

Those who met the Hansens at the docks greeted them with tears of rejoicing. Wonderful testimonies abounded of all that God had done during their absence. God had been working marvelously in the lives of those Chinese believers.

On March 21, 1928, little Harold Jonathan Hansen was born. How thrilled Letta was as she held her little son in her arms. Little Gwendolyn beamed at her new baby brother. After the birth of the baby, the Hansens settled back into a routine. Letta juggled her two children and the ministry she was involved in. Both Letta and Harold thought it best to communicate in Mandarin at all times. This continual practice of the language brought great improvement in their command of the language.

The political situation continued to be in an uproar. Chiang Kai-Shek had captured the capital of Peking and renamed it to Beijing. The Nationalists established China as a republic and declared that China would become a strong nation. There was talk about setting up a strong government, and yet fighting continued in many of the provinces. Communist troops which had once helped Chiang Kai-Shek were now in opposition to his leadership. They felt betrayed by him, because when he had taken over Shanghai, he broke with the communists and killed a large number of them who were amongst his followers. Indeed these were troubled times. If Letta looked at what was happening around her with a natural mindset, she would have packed her family up and fled back to the safety of American soil. The Hansens chose not to see things in the natural but to keep their eyes on Jesus.

Despite the turmoil, ministry had to go on. The Hansens knew there were souls to be saved and lives to be touched. They couldn't be sidetracked by what was going on around them. God continued to amaze Letta by opening many new doors. He set up plans and opportunities for ministry. One door that the Lord miraculously opened for the Hansens was the door of orphanage evangelism.

A few years before, a man dying of tuberculosis had come to the mission for prayer. He was from a church that didn't believe in healing, but he heard that the Hansens were used by God in miraculous physical healings. After prayer, he left and never returned again.

Out of the blue, many years later, a lady with a thirteen-year-old son came to see the Hansens. She asked to speak with Rev. Hansen. When he asked her what the problem was, she explained that her son was dying of tuberculosis. She went on to tell the Hansens that she was the wife of the man whom they had prayed for many years before. As a result of that prayer, her husband had been healed, and now she wanted prayer for the healing of her son.

Her son was saved, but five days later he slipped away into eternity to be with his redeemer. The mother returned to the mission and told the Hansens that she wanted to thank them for their kindness and love. She was the matron of a Buddhist orphanage. Through her, the Hansens were able to go to the orphanage and minister to the girls who lived there.

Letta enjoyed going to the Chinese girls' orphanage to spend time with the girls there. On every visit the children surrounded her, giggling and talking simultaneously. They eagerly waited to hear her many stories about Jesus and His love. She led eight of the girls to new life in Jesus. Each visit brought more girls into the saving knowledge of Jesus Christ. From all her visits a total of twenty girls accepted Christ.

When it was Chinese New Year, the girls received permission to go and visit with the missionaries. Twenty girls received the baptism of the Holy Spirit. When they returned to the orphanage they were on fire for God as never before. They witnessed fervently to the others in the orphanage. It wasn't long before the number of those saved had reached a hundred.

Unfortunately, the orphanage had to be closed down and these girls were sent away to other orphanages. Dividing the girls up in groups, they were sent on their way. One girl was sent alone to a new orphanage. She wrote constantly to the Hansens. She felt alone and poured out her heart to them in her letters. They in turn wrote her words of encouragement.

Another year rolled by, and when it was time for Chinese New Year again, the Hansens decided to spend some time visiting the little girl. What a wonderful blessing they received when they met with her. They found out that she had been forbidden to read a Bible or to sing from a hymnal; but nonetheless, she had won ten little children to the Lord. These children sat together out under some trees and quoted scriptures that the little girl had taught them. They prayed together consistently. One girl had touched the lives of ten other children. It amazed Letta to think of how one life could make such a great difference. She wondered about all the other children who had been sent out to the other orphanages. How many other souls were being touched as a result of their lives and testimonies?

Not a day went by that Letta didn't rejoice in what God was doing in her life and in the life of her family. She watched as baby Harold grew into a sturdy toddler. Gwendolyn and Harold, Jr. enjoyed playing together and keeping each other company. In the middle of 1930, Letta shared the joyous news with her husband that she was pregnant once again. He couldn't be more delighted. How his heart was overwhelmed with the fact that in his later years   of life he was being blessed with such a wonderful family.

On January 17, 1931, at two o'clock in the morning, a quiet hush engulfed the city of Peking. In the midst of the quiet, the Hansen's two-story red brick house, situated on the west side of the city, was filled with great excitement. Birth pangs had started and Rev. Hansen was pacing the floor. At 5 a.m., baby Margaret Belle Hansen joined the Hansen family. Both Gwendolyn and Harold Jr. were excited about having yet another sibling to play with.

Two-and-a-half-year-old Harold Jr. rushed into the room asking, "Where is my new baby bruvver?"

Instead of a baby brother, he was introduced to a baby sister. Five-year-old Gwen brushed past her little brother and informed everyone that she had come to take care of the new arrival.

Harold Jr. gruffly informed Gwen that she could have the new arrival, because he only wanted a brother!

"But mommy," he said, "I wanted a BOY; why did you have to have a girl?"

Both Letta and Rev. Hansen laughed. What a delight their children were to them.

Little Margaret Belle grew quickly, and her big, round blue eyes were a topic of amazement amongst the Chinese workers. One Chinese cook would mutter that those blue eyes followed him everywhere he went.

As for the childhood diseases, the Hansen children had their share of

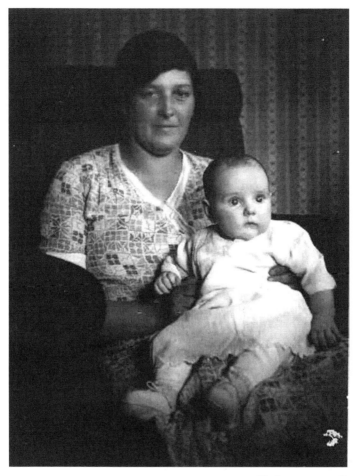

Letta and little Margaret Belle

them. Little Margaret Belle succumbed to all the diseases a child could have, including two bouts of Scarlet Fever. Each time she fell ill, prayers were offered up and she would miraculously get better. During her second bout of Scarlet Fever, the fever went very high. When Margaret had gotten better, Letta was combing Margaret's hair when the comb caught a snag, pulling out her entire head of hair. Seeing what had happened to her daughter, Letta was horrified. She was sure that little Margaret would grow up bald, but after much prayer, all her hair grew back with no problem.

From left: Harold Jonathan, Harold Hansen, Gwendolyn Hazel, Letta and Margaret Belle

Letta's hands were full with her three children to take care of and her various ministry involvements to attend to. Prior to their two-year furlough, the Hansens had been very involved with ministering in the prisons and amongst the police force. Since their arrival back in China, a new door was opened which allowed them to have unlimited freedom in ministering to the inmates of all the jails in Peking. Both Letta and Rev. Hansen were thrilled with this new avenue of evangelism. They joined with some local workers from different Pentecostal missions and went into the jails to hold meetings. Two of the largest prisons in Peking opened up their doors to the ministry teams.

After a few months of meetings, 42 prisoners were baptized. Although these people were in prison, their souls were free in Christ. The verse found in John 8:36 took on a fresh meaning: "If the Son therefore shall make you free, ye shall be free indeed." A short time later, another thirty-seven prisoners were baptized.

The prisoners were baptized in a tank made out of galvanized sheet iron that measured 3' x 3' x 7'. This container was carried easily to the prison, and the prisoners themselves used their wooden buckets to fill it up with water. Considering that baptism by immersion is symbolic of death to the former self, it was symbolic to use a tank that resembled a coffin.

In the midst of this revival, other prisons heard of the positive effect of the evangelism. There were other offers for Rev. Hansen to go into more prisons. One prison had about 500 prisoners, and they threw open their doors for evangelism.

At the beginning of one of their prison services, a young man interrupted Rev. Hansen and begged to be allowed to say something. He stood up before his fellow inmates and began to share his testimony.

"A short time ago I was privileged to be in the gang that worked on the outside, and I liked it very well. Not many days later the guard came to me and said, 'They are short a man in the kitchen. You go and help the cook.' This was indeed sad news for me, as I enjoyed working on the outside, especially in prison work.

After a few days I said to the cook, 'I hate to be in the kitchen, and I cannot understand why the guard forced me to come here.' The cook said to me, 'Why don't you tell the guard that you are sick so that he'll send you to your cell and have another man take your place, and in that way you will be put back on the outside again.' For several days this was running through my mind, and finally Satan got the victory over me, and I sent for the guard and told him I was sick. He said to me, 'Go to your cell and lie down.' This I did, and after a short time I was seized with terrible cramps. As time went on the pain became worse so that I couldn't stand it. Someone passing by my cell heard my moans and notified the guard, who in turn sent for the prison doctor. When he arrived I could hear him saying, 'He will not last long'; I wanted to explain what had happened but I couldn't speak for the pain. In my heart I prayed unto the Lord to have mercy on me, asking that if He would heal me this one time, I would confess what I had done. In a few minutes the pains started to leave me and before long I was well again.

This is the first opportunity I have had to make my confession. Dear

Friends, listen to me: Do not give place to the devil, as I did, but take your lot as you find it, and God will keep you. Thanks be to God who hears and answers prayers."

The eyes of those listening filled with tears. Even the most hardened listener was overcome with what this prisoner had shared. God used his testimony to reach out to all those who heard the message, and they streamed forward to receive new life in Jesus.

As the months rolled by, the prison ministry continued to expand. The power of God touched the lives of those on whom society had given up. Rev. Hansen's compassion for the lost never ceased to amaze Letta. Other people mumbled about how he was wasting his time with these misfits of society, and yet Letta knew differently.

The earlier converts from the prison went to Bible school after their release from prison. Now those ex-convicts ministered right alongside the Hansens, spreading the good news of Jesus to their fellow men. The ones still left in the prisons worked hard spreading the Good News to their fellow inmates. By the early part of 1931 there were over 228 prisoners who had accepted Jesus Christ and followed Him in water baptism.

The prisoners were not only ministered to in their spirits, but also in their physical needs. When Christmas time approached, the Hansens took the opportunity to make sure that the prisoners were given a tasty meal. The money for the food had been raised through the Missions Department of the Assemblies of God, and over 2,000 saved and unsaved prisoners were fed.

Normally the prisoners received only two meals a day consisting of corn flour steamed into bread with some salted Chinese cabbage or spinach. They never had the privilege of eating meat. On Christmas Day Letta watched with quiet joy as the prisoners' eyes sparkled when they received their wonderful meal of meat and rice and vegetables. In the spiritual realm captives were being set free, but in the natural realm fighting continued to surround the Hansens during this time period in China's history. People were being brought into captivity. The Japanese army moved into Manchuria and took control of the region. They were intent on coming against Chang Kai-Shek and the Republic of China. The northeastern provinces of China

Baptism in a tank made out of galvanized sheet iron

were in the midst of constant fighting and trouble.

Each morning brought more disturbing news about the ferocious fighting surrounding Letta and her family. Despite the troublesome times that surrounded them, Letta would wake her family up each morning for a time of devotions. They would read the Bible, and then they would pray for the safety of the nation and those missionaries who were in outlying, remote areas.

Letta didn't have time to be worried. God had given her so much to keep busy with, and she knew she needed to attend to the work He had put into her hands. As she took care of His work, surely He would take care of her family.

How exciting it was to be involved in God's work. Letta never knew what to expect from day to day. Her God was a God of the impossible, and no situation that faced her proved to be too difficult for Him to handle. A young girl who attended the Sunday school meetings showed signs of epilepsy. Her epileptic attacks increased, causing her great distress. Her parents brought her to the Hansens for prayer, and as the Hansens joined together and prayed against the attacks, the spirit of God reached down and touched the little girl, and her attacks stopped abruptly. Everyone rejoiced, and the healing became a testimony to the little girl's family of the miraculous healing power of the almighty God!

Two other girls in the Sunday school came to a decision to accept Christ and wanted to be baptized in water. They had faithfully attended Sunday school and opened their hearts to Jesus. It seemed so natural that they would follow Jesus in the step of baptism. The two young girls went home to ask their father's permission.

Mr. Lee, the girls' father, had to raise the girls alone due to his wife's unfortunate death several years before. He was protective over his children, and as they laid out their request before him he felt a sense of alarm. He had only heard rumors of this 'foreign religion,' but he didn't like what he had heard. After the girls finished their appeal, he just sat and stared at them. After what seemed like an eternity he responded gruffly by telling them they were not to go through the baptism. Both girls pleaded with him only to have him become all the more antagonistic. He rose up and forbade the girls ever to attend the Sunday school again.

Letta sent one of the leaders of the church to go talk to the man, making an attempt to change the stubborn father's mind. When the church leader arrived at the man's house and mentioned what he was there to talk about, the father rose up in anger, refusing to discuss the matter.

"My girls will only get baptized when I myself am baptized!" He shot out at the "Bible man" who had come to speak with him. He leaned back smugly, assured that he had finally closed this topic of discussion forever.

The disappointed girls did not give up on their desire to know more about their Jesus. They arranged with another child in their neighborhood, who was also attending Sunday school, to come home from Sunday school and teach them the lessons each week. So they continued with this arrangement, and before long there were several other children who would join the two little girls in their garden to listen to the child who had been to Sunday school. They continued to grow in their knowledge of Jesus.

Over the next few months the "Bible man" continued to visit Mr. Lee. Although he didn't see a change in Mr. Lee's attitude towards the Gospel, he did not give up praying for him. Late one night this Christian leader woke up with a start. He immediately sensed in his spirit that he was to go and see Mr. Lee, but it seemed illogical to do such a thing since it was late in the night. He attempted to fall back to sleep, but the urgency to get up and go to Mr. Lee's house would not go away. Finally he clambered out of bed and went off to see Mr. Lee. He knocked on the door of the house but there was no response. He wanted to give up and go home when he noticed a wisp of smoke escaping from the window. Rushing to the nearby water hole, he grabbed a pail and drew some water. Setting the pail down, he crashed down the flimsy front door of the house. He quickly grabbed the pail of cold water and rushed into Mr. Lee's bedroom only to find his padded coat on fire. As quickly as possible he doused Mr. Lee with the freezing water.

Sputtering, Mr. Lee woke from his sleep. He yelled furiously at his unwelcome visitor and demanded to know what he was doing. It didn't take long for the man to explain himself and for Mr. Lee to realize that he had been saved from burning to death. He had fallen asleep while smoking a pipe and the pipe had dropped onto his padded coat. All his bedclothes were on fire, and he wasn't even aware of it because the fire had just begun to reach his flesh. He asked the Bible man how he knew to come at this strange hour and when he learned that it had been God who told him to come, Mr. Lee fell to his knees before God. He begged the man to lead him in a prayer of repentance.

The next week Mr. Lee and both his little girls were baptized in water. How the church rejoiced at the miracle God had done. The girls were overjoyed that they were now joined by their father in their newfound relationship with Jesus Christ.

God's power continued to work marvelously amongst the Christians in Peking. Even those in the military came to hear of the Good News. The times were unstable, and the Chinese were longing for an answer to life and its problems. When the people entered the churches, Jesus met them at their place of need and their lives were stabilized once again. Where these people had no peace, Christ came and gave them HIS peace, which the world couldn't comprehend.

One day a taoist priest came to the church; he had come from the largest Taoist temple in Peking. He began to attend faithfully, listening to everything that was said. He longed for peace. All his life he had been striving for a real inner peace. He had tried for years to follow paths of balance between good and evil, but now he was at a time in his life where he knew the path he had taken was not leading him to a place of peace. He made the decision to follow Jesus Christ and become a new believer. What joy filled his heart as he realized that finally he had found the peace he'd been searching for!

With the increase in converts, the Hansens made more trips out to the villages. So many wanted to hear the Gospel, and Jesus' words rang true:

"The fields are white unto harvest, but the laborers are few."

The workers were stretched to the utmost attempting to reach all those who were hungry for the truth. Trouble in the villages increased day by day, and when Letta went out to the villages she never knew what she would have to face. Before each outreach, Harold and Letta knelt to pray to get the mind of God as to whether they should go or not. They knew they had to rely totally on the leading and direction of the Holy Spirit. Letta was assured she had nothing to fear as long as she was doing what God wanted her to do. She knew if she were where God wanted her to be, He would be in control of every circumstance or situation she found herself in.

In the middle of 1933, Harold told Letta she would need to pray regarding a missionary journey they needed to make.

"Where are we going?" Letta asked.

"We have to go to Inner Mongolia to spend the summer," Harold responded. "I know that this is a great thing I am asking of you, but I also know that God will go before us if He wants us to go."

Letta prayed and received peace in her spirit. The next few weeks were filled with the task of packing up in preparation to leave on the trip. The children bounced off the walls with excitement! Naturally they couldn't

Trip to Mongolia

comprehend the dangers that lay before them — all they could think about was the new adventure they were embarking on. It warmed Letta's heart to see the way her children were so eager to go.

"Oh, Father, if only I could be more like these children. They have no fear of the future or of what is surrounding them. God, give me this same child-like faith. I need you to strengthen all of us at this time. In the name of Jesus, amen."

The first leg of the journey was from Peking to Kalgan (Changchiakou). The Hansens spent three weeks ministering at two mission stations in that area. The whole city of Kalgan was under military rule. During the three weeks of their stay in that area, they saw God's hand of protection upon them.

From Kalgan they set out for Changpei Hsien. Although this was just thirty miles away from Kalgan, the journey was not an easy journey. They had to travel up a dry riverbed lined with cobblestones. Two-wheeled carts pulled along by mules carried their belongings. The dry riverbed ended at a narrow mountain road filled with potholes. The holes were so deep that if the wheel of the cart fell in, it would upset the whole cart. The tedious journey took over thirteen long hours.

Not only was the journey harsh with the condition of the road, but also those in the group knew that they could come face to face with a gang of bandits at any time. Bandits infested the path they were traveling on.

Exhaustion clothed every member of the group. The children no longer thought of this as such a fun adventure.

"Mommy, when will we get there?" "Mommy, I'm tired; I want to go back home!"

Letta just plodded forward, assuring the children it would not be long before they reached their destination.

What a relief it was to come up over a hill and see Rev. Hindle standing outside the mission chapel waiting for them. Rev. Hindle didn't know when they would be arriving, but as he was praying in his chapel, God impressed upon him that he should go outside and wait for the party as they would be arriving soon. For the group of mission workers, Rev. Hindle seemed almost like an angel sent by God. Their hearts rose in courage to see how God had gone before them, preparing the way and protecting them during their rough journey.

Letta gazed across the plain that surrounded them. She could see farms everywhere. What a difference this was compared to where they were staying in Peking. Her heart leapt to see the opportunities that lay before them. There were so many souls waiting to hear the Good News. She was impressed at the sacrifices Rev. and Mrs. Hindle were making to stay in this remote area.

During their stay at the Changpei Hsien outstation, they held meetings daily. The chapel filled up quickly at each meeting. Hearts were hungry to hear the Good News. These villagers had been experiencing terrible attacks, and they knew that nothing could help them except Jesus.

Rev. Hindle had organized a baptismal service in which seven were baptized. Of those baptized, there was an older woman who had heard the Gospel many years before through a missionary called Mr. Gilmore. Mr. Gilmore had been a pioneer missionary to Mongolia. Now, all these years later, this woman was dedicating her life to Christ and following Him in water baptism. Rev. Hansen couldn't help but be overwhelmed to see the outcome of a seed that had been planted many years earlier. It encouraged his heart to see that often we may not see the fulfillment of the work we do, but God's Word is true and it will not come back void. Letta and Harold Hansen determined to be all the more diligent in planting more seeds of the Good News all over Northern China.

The Hansens traveled to outlying areas, holding meetings in each village. The villagers packed out all the services. In the village of Shang Tu Hsien, in particular, many of the city officials came for the meetings. They were determined to follow after Christ. This city was in a strategic location to be used as a springboard to push the Gospel into the regions surrounding it.

After just a few days, they had to pack up once again to continue their journey to Gashatay. The journey took two full days, across more bandit-infested lands. Once again, the Lord protected them and they made it safely to their destination.

Coming up over the hill, they looked down to see the mission station of Gashatay. The scene before them resembled a village. There was a chapel surrounded by some small mud houses where the missionaries stayed. Other buildings stood off to the side; these were used for a school. Weary with travel, the Hansens took a couple days to rest. After their time of rest they joined in helping with the various meetings being held.

The summer months moved along quickly.

All too soon, the time approached for the Hansens to make the journey back to Peking. They were sad to have to part with the Hindles. God had knit their hearts together during this joint missionary endeavor. They prayed together and encouraged the Hindles to keep serving the Lord. The Hindles had been ministering in that region for twenty years, and God had blessed their labor.

On the way back down to Peking, their trip appeared to go faster. They stopped along the way to rest and hold meetings. In some of the missions, there were people baptized in the Holy Spirit. Baptism in water took place in every meeting. Before they knew it they had arrived back home safe and sound.

After a short time of rest, they jumped right back into their busy schedule. Rev. Hansen made his rounds of the prisons and was delighted to find that those who had been taking care of the work in his absence had done a fine job. More souls had come into the Kingdom and had been baptized during his absence.

The chapel where the Hansens held their main services had filled to overflowing. On January 5, 1936, Letta saw 24 people baptized in water. Some of those baptized were from their outstation work in Chenfu. Spiritually things couldn't have been better. Lives were changing and people were rejoicing in their newfound salvation. However, in the natural, turmoil continued to escalate. Wars and rumors of wars abounded. No one knew what the next day would bring.

In the midst of this uncertainty, Lois finished Bible school and was to be married to a fine young pastor. This truly was a joyous occasion for Letta, as she watched her adopted daughter embark on a journey to build her own family. Truly Lois had been a gift to Letta at a time she needed comfort.

In the middle of 1937, the Japanese and the Chinese had a clash at the Marco Polo Bridge in North China. This incident marked the beginning of the end of the Japanese war of oppression against the Republic of China. Each day situations worsened and problems increased. A request came urging the Hansens to return to the United States for a furlough, Letta felt mixed feelings about leaving China. On the one hand she was excited to go back and visit with her family. Her family had never met her two youngest children, Harold Jonathan and Margaret Belle. On the other hand, she felt sad to be leaving her Chinese friends. No one could know what would happen while they were away.

When the Hansens left on their voyage back to the United States, there wasn't a dry eye among them. Harold Jr. and little Margaret were leaving the only country they had known. This was a time of change for all the Hansens.

Years before, the Hansens had agreed to converse in Chinese even within their home. Thus, their command of the Chinese language had improved greatly. The older two children, who were already of school age, went to the American school in Peking and had become fluent in English. Little Margaret still was communicating only in Mandarin. She could understand English, but refused to use it. All her little friends were Chinese or other missionary children, and so they communicated with one another in Chinese.

Once the Hansens had arrived in the United States, the relatives tried to talk to little Margaret in English, but she refused to respond. She glanced over at her mother answering the question in Mandarin. Letta translated Margaret's answer into English. However, it wasn't long before Little Margaret found it much easier to talk in English, and she began to use it fluently.

Letta thanked God daily for how flexible her children were. God had blessed her with three wonderful children. They were ever willing to enter into whatever work their parents asked them to do. They enjoyed learning more about God and sharing what they knew with others. Now that they were in the United States, they didn't waste any time getting to know their many relatives. What a joyful time God gave them during this furlough.

Letta hadn't realized how much she needed this time away from the stress and strain of war-torn China. However, being away from China didn't mean she forgot those laboring on in the land of China. Thousands of miles distanced Letta from the fighting and the problems in China, but her heart never lost the burden to pray for that nation. Her ears were ever tuned to any news that might come in about the situation and circumstances in the land of China. She could not let go of the burden that God Himself had planted so deeply within her heart. She knew it would not be long before she and her family would return to China and continue the work they had left there.

7

October 1938 arrived and the Hansens were ready to return to China. Despite the troubling reports of the Japanese occupation in China, they still needed to return to the field. In the midst of planning their return trip, they realized they didn't have sufficient funds to pay for their passage back to China. Together, Letta and Harold Hansen knelt down and prayed. They lifted up their petition before the Father asking Him to provide their needs.

This wasn't the first time they had come to Him in prayer in regards to their finances. They had seen Him provide time and again in the past. and they had the assurance that this time would be no different.

After prayer, they began making the necessary arrangements, by faith, to leave Seattle on October 14, 1938. God honored their step of faith, and someone contacted them and gave them the sufficient funds to make the trip back to China.

The trip back to China was not uneventful. The ship they were on hit bad weather while out at sea. For two days and nights the steamer was tossed to and fro in a typhoon. Letta was reminded of her first voyage to China on which she had gone through a similar gale. God had protected her on that voyage, and she knew her heavenly Father would protect her family during this journey as well.

Early one morning, the crashing of the waves on the side of the vessel woke Margaret Belle up and she needed to go to the bathroom. There was no attached toilet in the cabin, so Letta had to accompany Margaret Belle down the passageway to the common bathroom.

Passengers had been warned not to open the storm doors that led out to the deck area due to the dangerous waves. As Letta approached the door a Jewish merchant opened the storm door and was immediately drenched by a great wave. After struggling to shut the door, he spun around only to see Letta calmly holding the hand of her youngest daughter and they walked along. The sight of her calm demeanor infuriated him. He reached out and put his two hands on her shoulders, shaking her as he yelled, "Why aren't you afraid?" Letta pulled away abruptly, but he kept clinging to her and yelling, "Why aren't you afraid? Don't you know we could die?!"

"Dear sir," she replied calmly, "I have no reason to fear, for the One who loves me is with me and will take care of me."

"What do you mean," the man demanded, his eyes filled with a mixture of fear and anger.

"I mean exactly what I said. There is no need for me to waste my time being fearful. If God chooses to take me at this time in my life, I am prepared to go. If He should choose to save my life, then I am prepared to serve Him as I have always done."

Letta assured him that God would take care of them. The man allowed her to pray with him, and he felt peace flooding over him. As a result of their meeting, the man brought three other Jewish merchants to Rev. Hansen and asked him to share the Good News with them. What the devil had planned for destruction and confusion, God had planned for good. Out of that storm God produced an opportunity for His Good News to be shared.

By the early part of November the ship had reached China. The Hansens were greeted with great rejoicing. Those who had "held the fort" while they were gone were thrilled to have the Hansens back. News was quickly exchanged on the wartime situation. One major result of the war was that the hearts of the Chinese people were open and hungry for the Gospel. God was doing a real work amongst the Chinese people.

A few days after their arrival, the Truth Bible Institute moved to a new location. There was a special celebration organized to mark the opening of the school's new premises. The two large lecture halls were jammed with guests and over a hundred students.

Letta glanced around at the students and remembered how it had not been very long ago when the idea for a Bible school was first birthed in their hearts. Now, as she looked around the facility, she saw that God had outdone Himself. The compound consisted of 127 rooms. There was a great potential for training of men and women to go forth and spread the Good News throughout the land of China. Rev. Hansen always felt strongly that the Chinese should be trained to rise up and evangelize their nation as it had never been evangelized before. God was fulfilling His desire for His people to be equipped to share the Good News.

The time was ripe for people to go out and reap the harvest. The Hansens' hearts grew heavy with a deep urgency to spread the Gospel throughout China. They could see that the hearts of the people were hungrier than ever before. The number of new converts appeared to be growing by leaps and bounds. One of the new converts, a Mrs. Kao, begged the Hansens to come and visit her home. She wanted them to talk and pray with her elderly parents.

Letta and Harold organized a day to go and visit Mrs. Kao. On the day they visited her, though, the relatives of Mrs. Kao met them at the door and began to hurl curses at them. When the Hansens attempted to enter the house, they were refused entry and were sent away with more curses.

Despite the opposition of the relatives, the elderly parents of Mrs. Kao made an effort to go to the Hansens' home. After Letta had shared the Gospel with them, they expressed their desire to become Christians. The determination of this elderly Chinese couple was admirable. They were willing to sacrifice the approval of their family members to accept Jesus Christ as their personal Savior. When they accepted Christ, they were turning their backs on years of tradition and family ties. They had not made the decision lightly. They had counted the cost and were willing to pay the price to follow Jesus, because they knew it was worth it!

In the fall of 1940, God graciously poured out His Spirit on Northern China. The Lord marinated His people in the Spirit. Only the Spirit knew that there were rough times ahead, and this was a time of preparation. Missionaries from different denomina- tions in various parts of China put aside their personal differences and began to meet together to pray.

A massive prayer meeting was organized in Kalgan. Missionaries from Mongolia and many other stations joined together in one of the largest gatherings of missionaries in North China. The cry of all their hearts was for divine anointing and direction during the difficult days that stretched out before them.

God knew what needed to be done to prepare the hearts of these people. From the beginning of the meetings until the end the Lord moved mightily through spontaneous healings. His Spirit swept through their midst, and those who had never received the baptism in the Spirit were suddenly filled with the Spirit. A sweet spirit of prayer invaded the place, causing the missionaries to forget about mealtimes. Prayer filled every part of their day, from morning till night.

The Spirit of God didn't stop moving with the close of that massive prayer meeting. The sweet Spirit of God continued to move throughout Northern China.

In Peking, people gathered together in prayer every afternoon from two o'clock to four o'clock. People from all over the city streamed in for the afternoon prayer meetings. Those who had been opposed to the baptism of the Holy Spirit now were eager for it. The cry on everyone's heart was for more of God.

Rev. and Mrs. Beruldsen, a couple who lived in the Bible School compound, graciously opened their home for the afternoon prayer meetings. About this time, God brought Brother Benson, a British Assemblies of God missionary, to lead the afternoon prayer meetings. Brother Benson had been in prison for nine months. He had endured sufferings that — humanly speaking — could not be endured! God had manifested HIS resurrection power in and through Brother Benson.

One afternoon no sermon had been given, but everyone just fell to their knees in heavy intercession. The children, who were playing outside, suddenly felt drawn to enter the meeting hall. They slipped in and fell to the floor and began praying as they had never prayed before. No one wanted to close the meeting that day. The service continued on through the evening and right into the night. The sweet presence of the Lord swept over the whole room. No one had any desire to leave. As they soaked in the presence of the Lord, they knew they were gaining new strength to face the difficult days that lay ahead.

Letta looked forward to the afternoon prayer meetings. The meetings helped strengthen her to face the horrors she saw each day. She had to see those who were arrested by the Japanese soldiers as they were paraded through the streets. The Chinese people were suffering miserably around her, and often she didn't think she could take another day of seeing the suffering. Despite the suffering in the natural, here God was graciously pouring out extra blessings in the spiritual realm. He was showing Letta that indeed His grace is sufficient for those who were going through great trials. Not a day went by that Letta didn't cry out on behalf of those suffering. She prayed for peace to settle down upon the war- torn nation of China.

Letta joined with Rev. Hansen to intercede for a way to minister to the needs of the people. God the Provider — the great Jehovah Jireh — caused funds to be sent to the Hansens. As soon as they had received the money they knew God wanted them to use it to help those around them. They bought food for hungry families and clothing for those who were cold.

One family had gone away from the Lord and during the time of suffering the Hansens went and helped feed the family. Letta went back to the family and brought clothing for their children. The family fell to their knees and wept. They couldn't understand how Letta could still be showing them love even though they had stopped attending the church meetings. They began to grasp the real meaning of unconditional love. Through this show of love and mercy, the family came back into close fellowship with all the other believers.

Another woman with five children had no money to feed her family. She felt she had no hope. She bundled her children up and marched them down to the river. She intended to end their lives in the icy waters of the river. God had other plans for her and stopped her from going through the terrible deed. As she stumbled back to her house, her heart continued to weigh her down. She wondered if she should have continued with her plan to end her life and the lives of her children. She tried to reason with herself that it would be more humane to die quickly rather than to starve to death slowly. When she reached her house, she saw the Hansens standing outside her door with food for her family. With tears streaming down her face she knelt before them to give glory to God. Christ showed her in a tangible way that He loved her and He was there for her.

There was no denying that the times were perilous. Many missionaries had already left China, but the Hansens knew they couldn't leave; somehow they knew that they had to be with the flock God had given them to oversee.

One night, as they were getting ready for bed, Harold turned to Letta and said, "I don't think the banks are safe at this time."

"If they aren't safe, what will you do?" She asked.

"I think I will take the money out of the bank and keep it in a safe in our home," Harold replied.

They prayed over this decision and agreed that this was what God wanted them to do. Almost as soon as the money had been removed from the bank, a law went into effect that froze every account in every bank; it didn't matter what amount of funds were in the account, and no one was able to withdraw their money from the bank. Indeed, once again God had given clear and precise directions.

Letta had always felt that she relied wholly on God for everything, but in these days of turmoil she realized she was being taken to a new level of trust. She clung to God for constant guidance and strength. Every decision she made, and in everything she did, she waited upon the Lord and followed only His leading and guiding. She knew her only security would come from relying on the arm of God.

The night of December 7, 1941, Harold fell dreadfully ill. His eye had become infected, and now the infection coursed through his body. Letta stayed up with him throughout the night. Early the next morning she made sure the children were ready to go to their school that was four miles away from the house.

The moment the children left the house, Harold was up and moving around dressing himself. Letta walked into the bedroom and saw that he was getting ready to go out.

"Harold, please go back to bed!" she begged her husband.

"It's alright Letta, I have no time to be sick."

"You just get right back into bed," Letta insisted. "You have been fighting that eye infection and you are not well enough to be moving around yet."

Finally he succumbed to Letta's pleadings and clambered back into bed. Letta arranged the blankets around him and encouraged him to try and get some rest while the children were at school. It wasn't hard for him to obey his wife's advice since his body was worn down with the infection.

As he snuggled down under the blankets there was a loud knock on the door. Mr. Ku, the old Chinese servant, scuffled to the door to answer it. When he opened the door, he was shocked to see Japanese soldiers standing in front of him.

One of the soldiers pushed his bayonet into Mr. Ku's chest and spat out, "MASTER!"

Mr. Ku didn't have to think twice about what the man wanted. It was obvious the soldier wanted Mr. Ku to take him to Rev. Hansen. He led the soldiers through the house to the room where Rev. Hansen was lying in bed. Letta was walking through the hallway and almost jumped out of her skin when she saw the soldiers enter the room. They shoved past Letta, leaving her gasping. Pulling herself together, she hurried after them into her bedroom. A guard spun around, grabbed her forearm forcefully, and pushed her back out the door. The door slammed shut with a resounding thud, leaving Letta shaking like a leaf on the outside.

Trembling she leaned up against the door, pressing her ear hard against it attempting to catch a hint of what was being said inside. The muffled voices of the soldiers drifted past the barrier of the door, and Letta thought she heard the soldiers questioning her husband about his furniture. Letta couldn't imagine what the Japanese soldiers wanted with her husband, but she knew that worrying would not help. Letta inched herself away from the door and stationed herself further down the hallway, and then she began to pray earnestly for her husband's safety. At this time there was no one who could help her except God Himself.

No one in the Hansen household had yet heard the horrific news that on that very day the Japanese had bombed the American military base at Pearl Harbor. After an hour with her husband, the guards pushed the door open and marched out. They gruffly informed the Hansens that they were now under house arrest. They were informed that if Rev. Hansen had been well, they would have taken him as a prisoner. Letta rejoiced at the wonderful workings of God. If her husband had not been sick that day, he would have been snatched from the family. She marveled at how things worked together for good.

The soldiers remained in the house waiting for the Hansen children to return from school. The children had gone to school totally unaware of the trouble which was about to fall on their family. On the way to school, the children saw Japanese soldiers lining the street, but this didn't alarm them. The Japanese had been occupying the city for quite some time. The soldiers only concerned themselves with the Chinese citizens and left the foreign residents alone.

After an hour in school, the children were summoned to the office. They hurried to the office where a teacher told the children to get their coats and rush home. Little Margaret didn't know what to think. Her young girl's mind raced with panicky thoughts, wondering what could be so urgent that they were called out of class and told to rush home. She wondered if her father's illness had taken a deadly turn. As she pedaled her bicycle home, her heart pounded against her chest and she prayed over and over again, "Oh, Lord, Please don't let my daddy die! Please don't let him die!"

The three children rounded the corner near their house and saw Japanese soldiers marching in front of their home. Margie's heart constricted with fear when she saw the soldiers with their bayonets standing guard in front of her own home. The children hopped off their bicycles, letting them fall to the ground in a loud clatter. They raced past the soldiers into their home.

"Mama! Mama!" they cried as they ran into the house.

Letta rushed to meet them, opening her arms wide for them. They tumbled into her arms and she pulled them close, like a mother hen hiding her chicks under her wings. They didn't have long to hug before the soldiers gruffly told them to stand at attention.

The children were told to line up against the wall and stand straight. Standing at attention the whole family was informed that they were now under house arrest. The soldiers went on to explain what it meant to be under house arrest. They would not be allowed to look out any of the windows. They were not to try and contact anyone outside the home. After these instructions, the soldiers shut the doors and sealed them from top to bottom with red paper.

The family just stood there in silence. The whole family was in a state of shock. They found it hard to fully comprehend what was happening to them. Suddenly the silence was broken with everyone wanting to talk at once. Each person tried to get some kind of explanation for what had happened. Letta calmed the children down by reaching for the Bible and reading to them. After they had read for a while they prayed together. The time spent in worship to the Lord brought a deep peace that helped them think clearly enough to set up a daily routine.

The Hansen's house was a two-story building; the upper floor was used for living quarters and the hall downstairs was used for church meetings. Five soldiers were left downstairs in the church meeting hall to guard the family. Another soldier was stationed outside the house. The soldiers did not appear friendly in the least, and the Hansens didn't want to do anything to test their patience.

The soldiers had warned the Hansens that they would be coming back for impromptu checks. Letta didn't know what these checks would entail. She didn't have long to wait to find out.

At the time of the first spot inspection, the Hansens were relaxing in the living room when the door burst open. Five soldiers and an officer marched in. They yelled at the family to stand at attention. It quickly became apparent that there was to be no talking or movement when the soldiers were doing their spot inspections. Harold Jr., or Bud as he was affectionately called, and Margie, although still young, quickly learned that this was not a time for fooling around.

Over the next few days, Japanese officers accompanied by four or five privates would enter the house without warning. The Hansens slept with their clothes on; it didn't take long to realize that the inspections happened in the middle of the night as well as in the daytime.

Soldiers had free reign of the house, day or night. They would walk through the house and take whatever they wanted. If the children made noise or fidgeted, they were given a quick poke with the bayonet. All faces had to look straight ahead; no one could say anything unless they were spoken to directly.

When the soldiers were not in the house, Letta and Rev. Hansen were discussing what they should do with the money that was in the safe. Some of the money belonged to the mission. They prayed together for the Lord to reveal to them a safe hiding place for this money — His money. After much prayer, they decided to hide the money in a safe and put the safe in an old cupboard.

On one of the spot inspections, a new group of guards marched in. The Hansens knew the routine and quickly found their places. Even Margie had learned to stand straight and tall, looking ahead without making the slightest noise. On this particular inspection, the officer in charge questioned Rev. Hansen about his finances. As he fired questions at Rev. Hansen, he was sitting directly across from the room where the safe was hidden.

Letta prayed silently in her heart. She needed for God to do a miracle. She wanted the officers to be blinded, just as the soldiers who had surrounded the Prophet Elisha's house in the Old Testament were blinded. She knew that if they found the money, they would confiscate it all.

Rev. Hansen tried to answer the questions as casually as possible. He was concerned because the safe not only contained money, but official mission documents and deeds to all the mission properties in Northern China. He prayed in his heart, "Lord, please protect that safe. Keep this officer from going into that room!"

Within moments, the officer looked up and said, "Enough for now!"

He and the soldiers marched out as suddenly as they had come in. Letta sighed with relief and the family joined together to praise God for His continued protection.

On another occasion the family was relaxing in the living room when the door burst open. They jumped up and darted to their positions. Gwen, who was sixteen at the time, was in another room washing clothes.

The soldiers glanced around the room but didn't seem interested in walking through the house as they normally did. The officer in charge fidgeted and looked around. Finally the soldiers said something to him in Japanese.

He moved from one foot to another, and then asked, "Where is one more girl?"

Letta called out, "Gwen! Hurry, the guards are here!"

Young Gwen ran into the room, drying her hands on her simple cotton apron. The officer's eyes drank in every move Gwen made as she crossed the room to take her place. Letta didn't care for the way he leered at her daughter, but she was powerless to do anything about it. Once Gwen stood in her place with her face looking straight ahead, the officer's eyes traveled slowly up and down her body.

He muttered, "Mmmm... a pretty girl, and nice age, just what one would want."

As his words sank in, Gwen's heart thudded against her chest like a drum. She forgot about the rules and she looked towards her mother, crying out, "Mama! Help me!"

Letta kept looking straight ahead. She calmly responded to her daughter, "Gwen, I can't help you. Now you have to allow God to help you. The God I have been teaching you about, you have to know that He is real."

"SHUT UP!" spat the officer.

The soldiers began to say things in Japanese. Although the Hansens couldn't understand the words they were using, they could comprehend the intention behind the words. They were taunting the officer to do something. The entire family prayed desperately in their hearts for God to intervene on their behalf. The officer became agitated and fidgeted even more. He spun on his heel and yelled out in broken English, "We go now! We come again another day!"

When the door closed on that group of soldiers, they never did return for any future inspections. God had protected Letta and her family once again. God had proved himself to be their protector. Not only was He their protector during their house arrest, but He was also their provider. He provided for them from unexpected sources.

The Hansens had helped so many people; during Letta's twenty years in China, she had ministered to needy families almost every day. One of the people she had helped was a woman from the church whose husband neglected the family's needs and spent any money he had on alcohol and opium. Over the years the Hansens had clothed the woman's children and made sure that they always had food on their table.

The tables had turned and now the Hansens were in need. They had no way of leaving their home. This lady would sneak by and risk her life to bring food to them. She was poor, and yet she sold whatever she had so that she could bring money to them. No matter how much the Hansens protested, she insisted on helping them.

"You have been kind to us all these years, and I want to help you now," she stated firmly.

Letta wept. She saw living proof of the Word of God. All those years the Hansens had cast their bread upon the waters, and now it was coming back to them. God had proven Himself time and again to be faithful in each and every situation.

During the second week of their house arrest, the soldiers came to inform them they would be allowed to move around the city. New rules were issued as to how they were to conduct themselves. Although they were permitted to travel throughout the city, they were forbidden to take an active part in the Christian work amongst the Chinese.

It was a relief to leave the house. The Hansens knew that their release from the house was not a real freedom. They still were under constant surveillance.

Groups of soldiers continued to burst into their home unexpectedly.

Gwen, Bud, and Margie went to their teachers' homes to continue their schoolwork.

As far as Christian work went, it frustrated Letta that she was not permitted to minister to the Chinese. She was grateful that at least they were allowed to attend the local church services. When they had petitioned to the soldiers in charge of their area for permis- sion, they had been kind enough to allow them the privilege of attending services as long as they made a report of the time of the service and the name of the pastor who would be speaking, as well as what he would be preaching about. They were even required to give the Japanese authorities a list of the songs that would be sung at the service. Although this seemed troublesome, she was glad that they had the opportu- nity to fellowship with other believers. In most other areas in China, the missionaries were forbidden from having any contact with other believers.

The Japanese army assigned plainclothes policemen to attend the church services. They made sure that the service was conducted according to the report submitted to the authorities. No foreigner was allowed to take an active role in the church service.

Outside of these tightly-regulated church services, the Hansens were forbidden from any personal ministry to the Chinese. They were not even allowed to visit the Chinese; if they spent too much time conversing with the Chinese, the person they were talking to would end up getting into trouble. Letta had to come to grips with the fact that her efforts to help actually would do more harm than good during these days of Japanese occupation.

She was not to be thwarted in her desire to help the Chinese believers. She began to take to her knees to intercede for them. She not only prayed for the Chinese Christians but she also prayed in earnest for the missionaries who were in concentration camps all across China.

Every day reports flooded in about how the Christians were being treated. Rather than allowing the reports to bring fear, Letta would fall to her knees and pray all the harder that God would give strength to the believers to go through these horrible times.

Other missionaries decided to get together to intercede for their Chinese brothers and sisters in Christ. The missionaries knew they were restricted but they also knew that no one could restrict the power of prayer.

Prayer meetings began in the Union Church. Missionaries from all denominations joined together for these wonderful meetings. The crisis around them had served as a catalyst to bring about unity. Each of them had the same cry on their heart; they just wanted more of God. Everyone longed for God to pour out His spirit over the land of China.

Communication outside of China was almost non- existent. When Letta wrote letters to her family in the United States, the letters were opened and censored. She learned to write without saying anything about the war situation in China. Letters from her family had been opened before they reached her, and parts of the letters were missing. Once again, the only thing she could do was pray.

Suffering draped around her like a heavy winter coat. Food became so expensive that people could no longer afford to buy even the most basic food items. Finances were tight since money was not allowed to come into the country.

One of the missionaries from the northern region came to visit and brought them word about a Chinese Christian worker in North China. He had received training in their Bible school and had proven to be a fine worker. He would go out preaching without even a cent in his pocket; he had great faith that God would supply his needs.

The Japanese had occupied the land ten miles on either side of the railroad line. The land outside of that was still considered Free China. The minister would travel out of the occupied territory and enter into Free China. On one of his trips the Red Army stopped him. They questioned him and then searched his pockets, discovering that he had money from Occupied China. The guerrillas immediately assumed he was a spy for the Japanese and they took him as a prisoner. Showing him no mercy, they dug a hole, threw him into it, and buried him alive.

Letta couldn't comprehend the wickedness that had been unleashed in China. She shuddered to think of the man's suffering. He knew his life was in constant danger when he crisscrossed China with the Gospel, and yet he was willing to risk his own life so that others could be saved. What a challenge that was to Letta's heart.

It wasn't long before the Japanese commandeered a public building. They used the building as a place to house their 'enemies'. The Americans were now their enemies. They would enter American homes and drag the men and boys away to be locked up. When the soldiers came to take Rev. Hansen away, they discovered that he was still too sick to be moved. The family rejoiced once again that they were allowed to stay together for a little while longer.

After a few months, all Americans in Peking were told to prepare to be evacuated. They had no idea where they would go. All they were told was to pack their things and be ready to leave at any time.

Letta received the news with mixed feelings. She had been miserable living in a constant state of tension, never knowing what was going to happen next. But what guarantee did she have that the situation would improve once they were evacuated? What about her children? What would happen to them in this move?

The orders were released that no one was allowed to bring furniture, so now came the problem of how to sell all the household goods. They found buyers for the furniture, only to be told they were not allowed to sell it after all. To the Hansens it seemed like they would be stuck with furniture that would just end up being left behind anyway. One Sunday, after church services, they went to their house and prayed together, committing the matter to God.

They said, "Lord, You know all about the future. Possibly there isn't going to be an evacuation. If we are to sell, then we need for You to send us the buyer.

If we are not to sell, then don't let us sell. You know the orders of the government. You know what will happen if we disobey. Shut every door You want shut. We want only Your will to be done."

With that simple prayer, they felt immediate peace. They knew God now had the matter in His hands.

The next morning, the Hansens' breakfast was interrupted by a knock on the door. Some people had come over to buy every single thing in the house. They were willing to pay a better price than any previous buyer had offered. The Hansens were elated and quickly sold the furniture. Every piece of furniture was removed from the house!

Early the following morning, some Japanese soldiers appeared. They had come to inform the Hansens that there was going to be an auction of all their furniture, but the Hansens were not home when the soldiers came. When they did arrive home that evening, they wondered what trouble they would face for having sold their household goods the previous day. They went to the Lord in prayer again and asked Him to help them out of this predicament.

The soldiers didn't return for a couple of weeks. When they finally did return they just looked around and said, "My, you are cleaned out. You don't have anything in your house."

No one even asked the Hansens when they'd sold the furniture. They were not questioned about the amount it had sold for. God took care of all the details. Once again, God had intervened on behalf of His servants. It was not easy for the family to live without furniture, but each day they praised God for allowing them to stay together as a family. It soon became clear they would not be evacuated as quickly as they had previously thought. Letta had to unpack all the trunks she had painstakingly packed.

The year was now 1943, and in the month of March, along with the pleasant weather and spring breezes, there came the news of the removal of all alien nationals from China. Could this be another false alarm? This time the Japanese seemed serious as they issued commands for American nationals to get their trunks and bedding ready to be picked up early on the morning of March 21st.

Bud's birthday would be on the 21st of March, and he felt so disappointed thinking he was going to be 'missing' his birthday. Letta decided to cheer him up by telling him they would celebrate his birthday on the 20th of March. It was imperative not to allow the negative situation surrounding them to affect their spirits.

March 21st arrived. The beds, bedding, and trunks lined the hallways in readiness. The heavy bags were taken away early in the morning. They just had a few small pieces of hand luggage left.

But then the departure date was delayed for three more days.

Everyone was told they were going to a Civilian Assembly Center (or more commonly referred to as an Internment or Concentration camp). Bits of information about the camp floated around Peking prior to the departure day. No one could be sure if the information was accurate; they had heard of others being taken from various parts of China, but no one had been seen returning.

Letta knew she had to write to her parents and let them know what was happening. This might be the last time she was able to write to them. Things had been so hectic, and she just wanted to sit and collect her thoughts. At first Letta just held the pen in hand and stared into empty space. She touched the tip of the pen to the paper, but then quickly drew it back. How could she begin this letter? Her heart was full of things to say and yet Letta knew she had to be careful of what she wrote. Finally, she put her pen to the paper and started the letter the only way she knew how.

Peking, China Mar. 21, 1943

Dear Mama, Papa, and all:

I hope Faith has received the letter I wrote a short time ago, if she has, I am sure you have read it too. Now things have changed; we are leaving our home and traveling to another part of the country. We take our bedding and clothing, the rest has been sold, you may know we have been busy trying to get every- thing settled. Now we are beginning to see the end.

The heavy baggage left this morning, we will leave in three more days. If this had happened in the beginning, I don't know how we could have stood it, but some way it doesn't seem so hard to stand now. We have found our faith is not imaginary but founded upon reality.

As we look back upon all that has happened in this last year and a half, we can't help but praise God for His wonderful care over us. Nothing has been nearly as bad as expected, and those things that have been hard, He has given grace to stand. When we were first notified of the change, I was praying and asking the Lord for strength and comfort – I received James 5:7–11 as my answer especially verse

I remembered Jeremiah when he was put in the dungeon, Daniel and his three companions, and as I thought, I realized they were not protected from suffering, but were given grace to endure, we too can expect special grace at this time. We read Hebrews 12 this morning and I found great comfort. There will be over 2,000 people in this place, so we will have a chance to do missionary work among our own people for a change. I hope you will pray for us, that we may be faithful....

Good–bye Mama and Papa and all, we won't be able to write again until after the war, but don't worry we will be alright, I'm sure, just pray for us as I know you will. I'm so busy I hardly know what I am doing. But can rest after we get started. So much love to you all, I'm so happy for Faith's letter.

Lovingly, Letta

When she signed the letter, Letta buried her face in her hands and cried. She longed for her parents. She loved them and wanted to be with them right at that moment. She knew this was yet another time she had to put her face forward to what was ahead. Unknown territory spread out before her, and God would once again take her through.

8

The morning of March 24th dawned. It didn't seem different from any other day, and yet this was the day they were going to be transported to Wei Hsien Camp in the Shantung Province. Letta scurried around dropping last minute items into open bags. A loud knock on the front door echoed throughout the empty house. Taking one last look around the room, she called out to the children. They moved toward the door where the soldiers were waiting to escort them to the American embassy.

When they stepped out into the street they saw over two hundred others who were already plodding along in a mournful silence. The Hansens fell into step behind everyone else. When they reached the embassy lawn, a Japanese policeman arranged everyone in groups and distributed numbers to each person. Their hand luggage was examined carefully. If the police felt that an item was too large or unnecessary, they would confiscate it. Everyone was told to pick up his or her bags and get ready to walk to the railroad station situated about a quarter of a mile from the embassy. To everyone's surprise and relief, two large trucks rolled up in front of the embassy and were quickly filled with the majority of the baggage. Once the trucks were loaded they drove away, and the prisoners walked solemnly out through the embassy gates.

Trudging through the streets of Peking the group presented a strange sight to the multitude of onlookers. Some looked on them with pity, wondering if they would ever be seen again. Others were too weak themselves to even care about the outcome of this group of expatriates.

Once at the railroad station, the soldiers pushed the Hansens and the rest of the group onto an already overcrowded platform. They merged with three hundred other "enemy" nationals. The Japanese soldiers paced up and down the platform directing people to the third class coach.

The prisoners were told they were going to a former Presbyterian Bible school that had been converted into a concentration camp. No one wanted to discuss the destination. They had no way of really knowing if that was going to be their true destination. There had been so many things they had been told over the past one and a half years, and many of them never happened. Letta knew their only security was God. He would not lie to them or lead them astray.

The trains bulged with prisoners who had already gotten on at other stations along the way. The soldiers shoved the prisoners into the jam-packed compartments. The prisoners piled their baggage on either end of the cars making room for the children to sleep up on the baggage racks.

The train jerked forward, throwing everyone on top of each other. Soon the engine fell into a steady rhythm. The three children were exhausted. The stale air in the compartments closed in on them, making them feel as though they were going to suffocate. Their lips felt dry and yet there was no water to wet them with. No one took the trouble to complain; everyone just wanted it all to be over. Letta could tell they were trying so hard to be brave. Her only solace was her firm belief that God had everything under control, and that He would give them the needed grace to go through this trial. The rhythmic sound of the wheels clicking on the track lulled the children into a fitful sleep. The journey was full of starts and stops but the conditions on the train stayed the same. The following day the train pulled into an unforgettable place – Camp Wei Hsien.

The motley group fell out onto the platform of the train station. The cool evening air caressed their hot skin. Guards herded them forward, prodding some of the slower ones with bayonets. Letta glanced over at her husband;

he was limping more than usual. She wished there was some way she could ease his pain. The arthritis in his knees had been giving him a lot of trouble. She whispered a prayer, asking God to continue to give them all strength to endure. They needed more grace to go on and face their future.

They trudged up to the gates of the camp. The fifteen-foot-high wall that surrounded the camp loomed overhead. Makeshift watchtowers rose up at strategic points along the wall. As they approached the entrance the huge front gates swung open ready to swallow them up. The sign over the entrance read "The Courtyard of the Happy Way." It was the former name given to the mission. The sign mocked the prisoners as they passed through the entrance.

The camp guards took over from the soldiers who had guarded them on the train. They shoved them up a hill past rubble and discarded school equipment towards a small athletic field. Everyone lined up on the field for a thorough check-up and roll call. Stomachs rumbled and bodies were weary with traveling. After the roll call, the group was marched over to Building #24 where the men were assigned to some basement classrooms and the females were assigned to the classrooms on a higher floor.

Letta moved quickly to claim some empty floor space for her girls. Her heart ached knowing that she had to be separated from Harold and Bud. Letta gathered and arranged the baggage in such a way that it surrounded them. They laid coats down on the cold floor. Letta dug through one of the bags and located some jackets. She carefully put the jackets around the children. They huddled together in a futile effort to keep warm with each other's body heat; but still the coldness of the floor crept up through their clothing and chilled them to the bone.

Just as they thought they were all settled, guards entered and escorted them out of the room. They were moved to large kitchen area where food was waiting for them. Some of those who were already residing in the camp had been assigned to prepare the food for them. Despite the fact that the meal was barely edible, the prisoners devoured every last morsel. The guards led the prisoners back to the large rooms and left them to settle down once more for the night. The coats and jackets were of little protection from the cold floor, but despite this hardship, their exhaustion from the rough train trip overcame them, pulling them down into a deep sleep.

The sun barely had peeked through the windows of the large hall when the soldiers came in to rouse the prisoners. No one had a chance to think of tidying up. They were forced to jump up and stand at attention. The guards yelled for them to vacate the rooms. Letta's hands instinctively went up to shield her eyes from the sunlight as she stumbled out the door of the building and into the open field. As her eyes grew accustomed to the brightness she glanced around at her surroundings. The bright daylight revealed the stark reality of her new "home." Letta remembered what she had written to her family.

"I remembered Jeremiah when he was put in the dungeon. Daniel and his three companions, and as I thought, I realized they were not protected from suffering, but were given grace to endure — we too can expect special grace at this time."

She whispered a prayer to the Lord, asking Him to give her the necessary grace to endure at this time. Her eyes darted about trying to locate Harold and Bud. What a relief, there they were, standing across the field with the men. They spotted each other at the same time and moved toward each other. They were ordered to line up and wait to be registered.

The registration process included signing a statement promising good behavior while living in the camp. They were also forced to declare whatever currency they had. That currency was then handed over to the authorities for safekeeping. The task seemed endless.

Standing in line waiting for their turn, Letta was able to get a good look around the camp. The camp had been a former Presbyterian Bible College established in 1884. The grounds covered about twenty acres. Different sizes and shapes of buildings scattered the grounds. Each building had rows of rooms measuring approximately ten feet by ten feet.

After standing for hours, they were finally given their room allocations. By the time they were assigned a room, they had learned many things about their new home.

They discovered that 1,750 prisoners were crowded into the facility. There were three large kitchens set up, and each kitchen was assigned varying numbers of people to feed. The amount of food distributed to each of the kitchens corresponded with the number of people each kitchen had to feed. Each kitchen was allo- cated to a specific group at the camp. The largest group in the camp numbered 750 people from Tsingtao. The second largest group numbered 600 from Tientsin, and the Peking group was the smallest of all the groups, with their kitchen having to feed 400 people.

There would be so much more to find out about the camp, but for the time being they needed to settle down in their new home. They had been allocated two rooms adjacent to each other. Letta could see there was much to thank God for. She heard from someone that if they had only four people in their family they would have had to squeeze into one tiny room. God had been merciful and faithful to them. They didn't take anything for granted and learned to thank God for every small blessing.

They wasted no time in getting their luggage put into their new rooms. All the prisoners' bedding and large trunks had been piled up carelessly by the guards, so now the prisoners had to rummage through the pile and retrieve what was theirs. Exhaustion and hunger plagued them. When the last of the bags had been dumped in the room, Letta rummaged through them and found the remainder of the food she had packed. She took it out and the family hungrily consumed every morsel.

Although exhausted, Letta knew she needed to get things set up. She moved about the rooms attempting to make them livable. Their belongings were sorted through and placed in convenient spots throughout the room. Letta carefully unpacked her delicate pieces of fine china. She decided that she wasn't going to save anything for a 'special' occasion, because she didn't know how many more 'special' times they would have left as a family. Each new day that the family was still alive and well and together was a special day! She wanted to celebrate each day.

The soldiers had assigned each person a number, and these numbers were marked onto a badge that each prisoner wore at all times. When

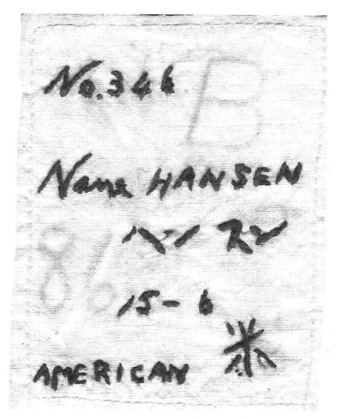

The actual badge worn by Letta

roll call was given, the entire camp would move quickly out onto a huge
football field. The prisoners stood for hours under the hot sun. The
guards meticulously checked each person's badge until they were satisfied
that everyone was accounted for. During one of the roll calls, the guards
announced that someone was missing. The prisoners had to stand for hours
as the guards counted and recounted them. If someone tried to sit down,
they were yelled at and jerked up to a standing position. The guards began
to yell at the prisoners, demanding to know who was missing. One of the
prisoners realized that the guards had made a mistake by not counting
the group leader they were questioning. When the mistake was brought to
their attention, they released the prisoners, who trudged back to their daily

routine, exhausted from the long hours of standing at attention.

The prisoners' daily routine was comprised of a self-implemented system. There was a prison committee made up of various prisoners. The committee set up rules for all the prisoners to abide by. The committee assigned a job assignment to each prisoner who was sixteen years and older. Anyone with a work assignment was required to work eight hours each day. With these various job allocations, the camp ran smoothly.

The committee worked hard to try and assign tasks according to the abilities of the prisoners. If someone knew how to cook, they were assigned a cooking job. If someone knew how to sew, they were assigned a job that related to sewing. There were big furnaces for baking bread, and some people were assigned the task of stoking the furnace. They had to always make sure there was fire to cook with.

People were assigned to be bread cutters. They had to slice the bread that had been baked. This task was done meticulously. Every loaf had to be sliced using the same measurement so that each prisoner received a fair portion.

Other prisoners were assigned to be part of the vegetable crew. A daily allotment of vegetables was given to the prisoners, but the Japanese guards would keep the food locked up until it became rotten. Maggots roamed freely on the meat and vegetables. When the vegetables were ripe with stench, the guards would release the food to the prisoners. The vegetable crew had to clean and sort through the vegetables. Picking through the slimy mound was not an easy task. Maggots wiggled their way lazily in and out of the vegetables. The crew painstakingly picked off the loathsome creatures and selected the vegetables to be eaten. The vegetables considered too rotten were tossed into a sickening heap. Needless to say, the prisoners in the camp didn't have much to eat. Their stomachs grumbled and complained of the emptiness within, but the condition of the Chinese people living outside the walls of the prison was far worse. Once or twice daily, the rotten food had to be dumped outside the walls of the camp. The vegetable crew made wooden boxes to store the rotten food in. The crew hoisted the wooden boxes up on their shoulders.

Guards with guns and bayonets walked alongside the crew as they went to dump out the food. The putrid smell of the rotten food invaded their nostrils causing the crew members to gag.

The starving Chinese would wait patiently for the gate to open up. Before the boxes hit the ground, they jumped on the boxes. They scrambled wildly to get as much food as possible. No matter how sour the food was, the Chinese would lunge for it. They used their hands to shovel the food into their mouths. No one bothered to think of taking the food home. They crawled over each other, clawing at the food and stuffing it into their mouths.

The prisoners on the vegetable crew would tell their fellow prisoners of the horrible sight outside the gate, and even though life within the camp was terrible, the prisoners realized that life outside the camp was even more miserable. At least with the working crews set up within the camp there was a semblance of order amidst the turmoil.

Aside from the cooking crews there were also workers assigned to pump water, whose job it was to stand for eight hours every day, pumping water for the bathrooms. The showers were organized so that each person was allowed two showers a week.

Anyone taking a shower had to line up and sign in before they were admitted into the bathhouse. The bathhouse consisted of two parallel rows of showers. One row of the showers was for the men and the other row for the women. Each person would stand under a faucet and the water would gush out onto the person taking a shower. Those assigned to pump water only pumped enough water for the allocated number of people per day. There was no such thing as dilly-dallying under the shower.

Rev. Hansen was one of the 'sanitary police' who would sit by the bathhouse with a file and check those who were entering the shower rooms. Each person had to be checked to make sure they were within their quota. If he found that they had already taken their quota of showers for the week, he would have to turn them away.

Other crews were assigned to dig holes for the toilets. The camp actually had some very modern toilets. The fixtures in the toilets were beautiful, but the pipes were not properly fitted. As a result of the lack of proper plumbing, the excrement overflowed the oriental-style toilet bowls. This presented a problem and the solution was to dig makeshift toilets. These substitute toilets were just open holes. When the hole would get too full, they would pile sand over it to close up the hole. If one of the holes didn't get filled up, it could be rather dangerous.

At one point there was an open cesspool. The weather was very hot and many of the people had prickly heat. Their bodies were covered with a rash of small red dots that itched terribly. A young Japanese-American boy had a very bad case of prickly heat. His mother had tried everything to no avail. The poor little fellow was running along playing one day when he fell right into the open cesspool. He struggled against the muck and mire. Someone saw him fall in and rushed over to drag him out. He flopped onto the ground in a stinking heap. He was scrubbed down thoroughly. They didn't attempt to salvage his clothes. New clothes were put on him, and he never had prickly heat again! It became quite a joke amongst the other prisoners. When someone had a bad case of prickly heat they were advised to go and jump into a cesspool.

The work crews were not just limited to those above the age of sixteen. Those under sixteen years of age were allowed to volunteer to help out in whatever way they could. Bud and Margie would go to the kitchen area to volunteer. When they showed up for duty they were given fly swatters. They went to the dining rooms and spent hours swatting flies. The flies covered the tables like a black blanket. The children would swat flies for one or two hours before the meal-times. The idea was to get rid of as many flies as they could before the people came in with their plates.

With all the new things to learn in the prison camp, the Hansens had their hands full. It wasn't long before they settled into a routine of sorts. Each of them had their separate job assignments, but Letta wasn't about to allow the new circumstances that surrounded them to deprive the family of time spent with God. She encouraged the children daily not to neglect their prayer time. As a family, they made a special effort to spend time in the Word.

Early each morning Letta would have a time of family devotions. After their devotion time, they would gather their porcelain plates and cups and walk over to the dining hall together and to line up for the meal.

Lining up became a part of life for everyone in the camp. They lined up for food, they lined up for taking showers, they lined up to use the toilet, and they basically lined up for everything.

After standing in the food line for what seemed like an eternity, they would reach the area where the food was distributed. The breakfast meal consisted of bread and water. On rare occasions the prisoners would get some tea, so they could have black tea and bread for breakfast. At noontime the prisoners would line up for stew cooked in huge iron cauldrons. Whatever vegetable and meat allotment had been given was dumped into the big pots and cooked as stew. The leftover stew from the afternoon was then watered down and made into soup for the evening meal.

When the prisoners lined up for their food, they would hand their plates to the person who had been assigned to serve them. No one was allowed to serve him or herself. Everyone had to be satisfied with whatever portion they were given.

Rev. Hansen stood well over 6 feet tall and had a large frame, but he was allocated the same amount of food as Letta with her 4'11" frame. Letta shared what- ever she had to eat with her husband. She made every effort to make sure he got enough to eat. Despite her sacrifices, Harold lost a tremendous amount of weight during the internment.

After getting their food, the adults usually moved over to some tables to eat. The children ran off to whatever spot they could find. Gwen, Bud, and Margie usually found a tree someplace out in the courtyard.

The prisoners lined up after the meals to have their plates washed. Etiquette teaches that it is improper to wipe one's plate clean. However, all etiquette from pre-camp days was tossed out the window out of necessity. The children soon learned that they MUST wipe their plates clean. One of the women prisoners painted several posters showing the camp residents how to use a piece of bread to wipe up every last bit from the plates. If a person didn't have bread, then they were expected to lick their plates clean. The reason for this new rule was to help conserve the water used for washing the dishes.

Each dish was handed to a person who quickly sloshed the dish in a big bucket of water, and then the dish was handed back to the prisoner as they continued to move along quickly in line. If each dish wasn't wiped clean after eating, the washing water would quickly become very dirty, and this posed a big problem to the limited water supply.

Back in the dining hall there were leftovers that needed to be taken care of. None of the prisoners were allowed to take the extra pieces of bread away from the dining hall area. The workers would go in after everyone had left and gather up all the leftover pieces of bread. They took these pieces of bread outside to be dried in the sun. Once the bread was sunned it was brought back to the kitchen where it was fried hard as a rock. These pieces of bread would then be used the next morning to make lumpy bread porridge. No matter how the food tasted, everyone ate their share because they knew that was the only thing they would get until the next meal. No one's appetite was ever really satisfied, and yet they thanked God that they had something to eat.

Children under the age of 12 were required to gather in the dining hall at specific times to line up for extra vitamins. The Red Cross had provided many of the vitamins but there were many minerals that were lacking. The camp committee set up alternate forms of giving the children their minerals. All the children had to eat ground up eggshells. The children were forced to stand in front of the crewmember and chomp away on the gritty shells. The shells felt like sand in the children's mouths and if they hadn't been forced to eat them on the spot they would have tried to spew them out of their mouths.

The young children needed eggs and milk, but those were items that were not allocated to the prisoners. Those in the camp had to come up with a solution for obtaining items that were not readily given to them. Some of the prisoners had money that they had smuggled into the camp. Those in the camp formed a black market ring. There were people outside with eggs and milk and various other items that those inside the camp wanted. Of course it wasn't easy to make a connection with those on the outside. There were guards patrolling the grounds at all times. The walls surrounding the camp had electrified wire running across the top. A young boy doubted that the wire had electricity. Unfortunately, when he tested his theory, he was electrocuted. Others were quickly made aware that the electric wire was the real thing.

The black market traders quickly set up a system to get past the guards. The old walls had holes through which the prisoners would drop a rope with a basket tied onto it. They would deposit some money in the basket and slowly lower it. The person on the outside would take out the money and replace it with eggs or milk or whatever other item had been requested.

The black market traders recruited the help of the younger children to act as lookouts for the guards. The children stood and played in their assigned area, and if they saw a guard coming they would sing a certain tune or whistle. The tune had to be loud enough so that the next child in the line would pass along the warning.

The punishment for trading on the black market was severe: it usually landed someone in solitary confinement. The solitary confinement area consisted of makeshift human kennels. Once a day, food was thrown in through a small hole near the top of the kennel. Another punishment often administered was having the person be pulled in four different directions. After a severe beating, the four guards took hold of the arms and legs of the prisoner and pulled as hard as they could. Despite these agonizing punishments people still took the risk of trading on the black market so that they could get extra food into the camp.

Life in the concentration camp couldn't be considered normal. Those who were forced to embrace this new lifestyle tried to make the best of it. As long as the prisoners obeyed all the rules set down by the Japanese guards, they were left alone. The greatest challenge was that the rules seemed to change on a daily basis. Letta and her family would drift on this sea of uncertainty for six long months, but her faith in God's promise to go before her and guide her through the rough waters gave her the assurance she needed that He would bring her family safely through this trial.

9

The many challenges that faced Letta in the camp forced her to cope with just surviving day by day. She had to live in a whole new dimension of faith, not only to give her life into the hands of the Father, but also to release the lives of her children into His faithful hands.

Letta's health deteriorated while in the camp. She had to be hospitalized in the makeshift infirmary for two months due to recurring heart attacks. Harold also faced serious health problems.

The Hansen children suffered as they watched their parents' difficult trials. Sixteen-year-old Gwen took over the roles of 'mother' and 'caretaker.' She made sure everyone had something to do to keep occupied. Bud kept busy finding ways and means to acquire much coveted food items through trade. Being the youngest, Margie found the suffering hardest to bear.

When Letta was admitted to the infirmary, twelve-year-old Margie wasn't allowed to go in to visit her. She longed to be close to her mother, but rules were rules. She prowled around the grounds of the infirmary looking for a hidden entrance. One day she discovered a window nestled in the wall high above her head. She figured out from the layout of the building that the window was in her mother's room. Standing below the window, she yelled up, "Mom, are you there? Can you hear me?" "Mommy, this is Margaret Belle. Mom, I love you!"

Letta smiled weakly as her daughter's voice drifted across the room. She longed to be with her little girl. How she wished she could leap out of the bed and go over to the window, but she didn't have the energy to respond. She prayed for all her children that they would be safe while she was cooped up in the infirmary.

Margie tried to make the best of her time in the concentration camp. The adults discovered she spoke impeccable Mandarin. They pestered her to help them with their intonations. She accommodated them whenever she could. When she wasn't helping with the language she played with her newfound friends.

On a particularly hot day, Margie and her friends stumbled upon the entrance to an air raid shelter in the infirmary compound. They decided to explore the cold dark tunnel to escape the sweltering heat. They inched their way down into the dark tunnel. Their eyes took time to adjust to the inky darkness. Feeling for the side of the tunnels they guided themselves further down into the darkness. Wooden posts lined the walls of the shelter on either side of the tunnel. The children discovered that in the middle of the eleventh and twelfth post the dirt wall caved in slightly near the floor. They crouched down on their knees and maneuvered themselves into the indentation. In this position they were hidden from anyone walking through the tunnel. This became their secret hideout. They would sneak down and sit for hours telling secrets and dreaming of all the things that they would do one day when they got out of the camp.

Camp rules changed constantly, and it wasn't long before the guards announced that the air raid shelters were off limits. The warning was accompanied with the threat of severe punishment if anyone was discovered down in an air raid shelter. The children didn't think anything of the edict. They thought they would be able to continue their secret meetings without detection.

Not long after the announcement had been made, the girls decided to meet down in their secret hideout. Creeping down into the tunnel, they made their way to their secret spot. Suddenly they heard a thudding sound overhead. They froze.

Margie's mouth went dry. She leaned towards her friends and whispered, "Let's go up and see what is going on up there."

Crawling cautiously towards the mouth of the tunnel, they craned their necks so that they could see out the entrance. Nausea swirled around in the pit of her stomach when she saw that half the camp guards were there playing tennis. She knew she had to move back to their hiding place, but her legs refused to obey any of the frantic commands her brain issued. Rolling her eyes to glance at her friends, she realized that she was not the only one experiencing this frustrating lack of motion. She managed to emit a desperate whisper through gritted teeth.

"We have to go back!"

The task was easier said than done. With hearts pounding like sledgehammers the girls crept back to their hiding place. All facades of safety had been ripped away, and now they felt vulnerable and afraid.

Huddled together, bodies trembling, they sat staring into the darkness. Words dried up before they reached their lips. They waited for the chance to escape.

Their hearts slowed down to a steady beat and then it seemed as though the sound of their heartbeat was amplified. In fact, it sounded as though it was coming from the entrance of the tunnel. Margie's eyes darted up towards the noise and to her horror she saw the source of the sound. A tennis ball was bouncing its way down towards them. Lumbering behind the tennis ball was a stocky guard. His eyes hadn't adjusted to the darkness, and every time he approached the ball, his heavy boots sent it rolling further into the tunnel. With every kick the ball inched closer to the petrified girls.

The guard clambered down on his hands and knees; he groped on the ground, attempting to locate the ball. Instead of grasping the pesky ball he pushed it closer and closer to the children's hiding place.

Margie's heart gave a magnificent leap and lodged up in her throat. Her entire body broke out in cold sweat as she grasped her clammy hands together. She clenched her teeth to keep them from chattering.

Margie sent up a silent prayer, "God, if you get me out of this mess, I will never disobey this rule again! I will never come down here again!"

No sooner had the prayer been said, Margie saw the officer's large hand close over the ball. He stood up and spun around, stomping away from the girls' hiding place. The sound of his boots mercifully faded away.

The children remained frozen with fear for the longest time. No one dared utter a word. They sat for what seemed like an eternity, waiting for the game overhead to come to an end. Once they were sure everyone had left, they ran up to the surface determined never to go back to that place again! Margie knew that she had come close to being taken to the dreaded guardhouse, and she was grateful for the reprieve she had been given as an answer to her desperate prayer.

Letta not only had Margie and Gwen's safety on her mind, but she was also concerned with Bud. He was a young teenage boy at the time, and camp life proved to be monotonous. Letta knew that in his pursuit to find something to occupy his time he could easily get into trouble. Her worries were not far off the mark.

One day while Bud and his friends were playing softball, the ball flew over the wall. A unified groan could be heard as the group on the field watched their precious ball disappear out of sight. Not one to back down from a challenge, Bud remembered that there was a ladder leaning up against the watchtower. He laid out a plan to recapture their lost ball. Bud was chosen to climb over the wall, and if a guard should show up, those on the inside of the wall would whistle the tune "Old Black Joe." They would keep whistling that same tune until the guard left, at which time they would switch to "Yankee Doodle."

The plan sounded good.

The teenage boys dragged the ladder away from the guard tower, climbed up the gun mount, and put the ladder over the wall. Bud clambered down the ladder and scrambled through the cornfield looking for the ball. He found the ball without much effort and was just about to throw it over the wall when he heard the familiar sound of "Old Black Joe" being whistled. He flung himself down in the midst of the cornfield with his stomach against the ground. Laying there trembling, he listened to the whistling. To his relief he heard the tune switch to "Yankee Doodle;" leaping up he threw the ball over the wall and climbed back up the ladder. The boys were ready to help him lift the ladder up and over and quickly put it back against the watchtower. As soon as the ladder was back in its proper place, Bud and his friends ran as fast as their legs could carry them away from the area. Letta's prayers had kept Bud from being caught and taken to the guardhouse.

The sinister guardhouse brought fear to all the prisoners' hearts. From the gates of the camp, one had to trudge up past the guardhouse to get to the camp. News spread like wildfire when someone was dragged down the steep slope to the guardhouse. All activity would cease as everyone gathered at the top of the hill waiting in silence to find out what happened to the unfortunate prisoner being punished. No one knew if the person would leave the guardhouse dead, alive, or maimed. Concern for each other unified them as they waited for the outcome of the prisoner. One day some children were playing in the church courtyard overlooking the guardhouse. They ran to the edge of the courtyard, peered down at the guardhouse, and yelled. Quickly they darted back away from the edge and broke into laughter. Margie and her friends strolled by and decided to join in the silly game. There didn't need to be a logical reason for playing the game, as it was just another way to fend off boredom.

The mischievous children dashed back and forth towards the edge, yelling and giggling. A guard, appearing from nowhere, looked up and shouted at the children. As they scurried away from the edge, Margie spun around and shouted back down at the guard. Although she couldn't understand what he said, she tried her best to mimic him.

The children soon grew weary of their game and slowly dispersed. There was a ball game being played in another part of the camp. Margie wandered over to watch the game. She smoothed her little silk dress and pulled her sweater tighter. Letta had told Margie it was okay to wear nice dresses everyday; there was no longer any reason for saving special things for special days.

A cool, gentle breeze caressed her cheek as she stood watching from the outskirts of the large ball field. The sounds of the players and those cheering the game lulled her into a peaceful mood. Suddenly a hand grabbed her by the nape of her neck, jerking her out of her reverie. The next thing she knew she was being dragged backwards across the field, her head bobbing up and down. Margie craned her neck around and caught a glimpse of the guard who held her. Anger distorted the man's features. He hauled her across the field and down to the guardhouse. By the time they reached the guardhouse, her silk dress had ripped right down the front.

Margie's mind fumbled around in an attempt to block out what was happening to her. She kept mumbling, "Mama won't be mad. She told me to wear my best dress. We don't have to save anything for special occasions."

Her body bumped roughly up over the wooden steps of the porch. The soldier tossed her through the doorway and Margie crumpled onto the floor. The guard reached over for a makeshift weapon of thickly rolled up magazines. With one swift blow, he struck her head. Her head jerked backwards and her hands flew up over her head in a weak attempt to shield herself from the onslaught of the blows. The guard lunged forward, bringing the weapon down on her time and again. He beat her head and her body continuously with all his might. Then suddenly the blows stopped as suddenly as they had started.

Like a frightened animal, Margie sat quivering in a pool of her own urine, staring blankly down at the floor in numbness as she heard the guard march out of the room.

Within a short time the guard reentered the room with a Japanese lady who was married to an American. Margie looked up in a daze. Her heart felt somewhat comforted to see this lady, as she had spent many hours babysitting the woman's little children. Having the woman there made her feel calmer and not so alone.

The guard looked over at the lady and spat, "You talk!"

A flood of Japanese gushed from his mouth. The woman endeavored to interpret for Margie, who still sat quivering on the floor. The guard accused her of being the leader of a gang. The translator spoke quietly, adding her own words of comfort.

Margie's eyes glazed over. Shaking uncontrollably, she plucked at the torn pieces of her dress. The man strode around the room waving his arms to emphasize what he was saying. She flinched at the slightest movement of his arms. Once the tirade was over, he dismissed the interpreter, reached for his improvised weapon, and beat her some more.

She didn't know when he stopped. He pulled her sweater over her head and shoved her out the door. She tumbled forward off the porch and collapsed on the ground. With quivering muscles she willed herself to stand up, but her legs would not cooperate. She slumped back down on the ground, her face falling forward into the dirt. Wrenching sobs shook her bruised body.

Gwen rushed down the hill towards her sister, scooping her up into her arms. Gwen was risking her life to approach the guardhouse. No one was allowed to leave the top of the hill, but she didn't care. Her little sister was in trouble and she had to help. She knew that she was putting herself in danger of being beaten herself, but at that moment the only thing that mattered was getting to Margie.

Margie's body went limp in her arms. Gwen dragged the dead weight up the incline; the task was too much for her to handle alone. She called out to several of the men to come and help her carry her sister.

Margie was delirious for three days. Tossing and turning in her bed, she would slip in and out of consciousness. Anytime she regained consciousness, she went frantic with fear.

Letta begged for permission to leave her bed so that she could take care of her daughter. She sat by Margaret's bed, brushing her forehead with a wet cloth. She traced the bruises on her daughter's cheeks and she wept. She wept because she had been cooped up in the infirmary when her baby was being beaten. She cried because she felt so helpless watching her daughter suffering.

"OH God, please forgive him, he doesn't know what he has done!! He needs you, just as I need you! Please help me God! Please help my darling baby girl, help her come out of this!"

The Hansens faced constant threats of harm and danger. Rumors of family separation and torture circulated around the camp, keeping everyone's nerves raw. Rev. Hansen's knees and ankles buckled up with arthritis. His condition worsened to the point where he was unable to rise up by himself from a bed or a chair.

Towards the middle of July 1943, the Hansens' weakened condition caused their names to be added to a list of people who would be exchange prisoners of war. Once again God had taken something that was seemingly bad and had turned it around for their good. Those on the exchange list were given the chance to take their names off the list and remain behind in the camp.

The Hansens were faced with a major dilemma. The Japanese had listed Bud as being of military age, and they thought if they were to make a statement in favor of leaving the camp the Japanese would somehow keep Bud in the camp. They submitted a statement refusing to leave the concentration camp. When the doctor found out what they had done, he urged them to change their statement. He persuaded them that there would be no way they could survive much longer in the camp.

Their statement had already been submitted, so now they faced the difficult task of retrieving the document. One of the young prisoners offered to go to the commanding officer to retrieve their statement.

He entered the office just as the officer-in-charge was stepping outside to watch a brawl. There piled on the desk was a stack of papers. Glancing at the top of the stack, the young man could barely believe his eyes. On the very top of the stack was the Hansens' statement! Whisking the paper into his pocket, the young man turned on his heel and hurried out.

God's hand of protection continued to cover the lives of the Hansens. Their time in the camp was fast coming to a close. They prepared themselves for their departure. When the family gathered together in their rooms, Rev. Hansen encouraged the children to memorize the numbers on his travelers' checks that had been cut diagonally and sewn into the lining of his coat. As the day for the exchange drew closer, he quizzed the children to make sure they could still remember the numbers from the travelers' checks. Margaret had memorized all the numbers on the traveler's checks and could recite them without any mistakes to her father.

A few weeks before the Hansens left, the children from the China Inland

Mission Chefoo School trudged into the camp to join those leaving. The prisoners ached as they watched the young children stumble into the center of the Wei Hsien Camp grounds. Most of them didn't have shoes, and their clothes were tattered and torn. They had no bedding. The rest of the prisoners rallied around trying to find bedding for the new arrivals.

Rumors permeated the camp as the departure date drew near. Every rumor insinuated that the exchange prisoners of war would never reach their destination. Letta refused to listen to the stories that slithered like poisonous snakes throughout the camp. Unfortunately, Gwen and Bud heard horrible tales.

"Mama, we heard that some prisoners were told they would be sent back to America, but they were killed instead!"

"God has NOT given us a spirit of fear!" Letta insisted. "If He has brought us safe thus far, surely He will take us the rest of the way." As always Letta kept her eyes on Jesus, the author and finisher of her faith. She knew there was no hope besides Him.

On September 15, 1943, the day for the Hansens' departure had arrived at long last. The morning dawned clear and bright. The family proceeded to their assigned kitchen area to have an early breakfast. After the breakfast, all those 'on the list' were told to meet at the assembly hall.

Letta and Harold could hardly motivate themselves due to their ongoing battle with illness. The children moved around the tiny rooms stuffing last minute things into their traveling cases. They lugged the few bags out the door and turned to take one last look around the rooms that had been their "home" for the past six months. Letta knew that her time spent in this place had been a training period and that she had grown by leaps and bounds in her faith, but of course she wouldn't miss this place. She was thrilled to be moving on!

The family made their way down to the assembly hall. Those whose names were on the list moved methodically into assigned positions. The Japanese soldiers spread out amongst the prisoners searching through everything. Grabbing books, they flipped through them and ripped up anything with writing on it. They allowed the prisoners to take their Bibles with them, but they made sure the cover pages on their Bibles were torn off. The soldiers ripped suitcases apart to uncover secret compartments hiding important documents. They searched the prisoners' clothing, and in their thorough search they discovered the travelers' checks carefully sewn into the lining of Rev. Hansen's coat. Thank God Rev. Hansen had the foresight to make his children memorize the numbers of those checks!

All anyone could think about was leaving the camp. For those waiting to be led away, it was as if they were in a dream. The time to be escorted out of the main gates finally arrived. They marched down the slope towards the main gate. The Hansens were the last ones in line. Letta moved slowly alongside the children. She had no strength to carry any of the bags. Harold could only walk with the help of a cane. His crippled knees hindered him from walking fast. The walk down the hill seemed to take forever.

Those prisoners remaining behind lined the walls and began to sing in unison. The camp orchestra joined with the voices of those lining the wall to bid farewell to the prisoners who had been chosen to leave. The beautiful sounds of "America," "America the Beautiful," and "My Country 'tis of Thee" filled the air. The songs buoyed the spirits of those moving towards the grassy banks of the little river that flowed just in front of the compound.

Those standing by the banks of the river looked up to where some of the prisoners were loading trucks with the heavier baggage. They drank in the sight of grass freshly moistened by morning dew. Off to the side some black and white cows from the camp dairy were quietly grazing. Although the brick walls of the camp rose up behind them, they seemed to be a million miles away. Men, women, and children lined the walls or stood on the higher ground within the wall. They continued to sing one song after another. The songs pushed aside their fears concerning the rumors and stories they had heard in the camp about the possible fate of exchange prisoners.

After a final roll call was made, the prisoners were herded onto the waiting buses. They squeezed into any available space, whether it was a proper seat or just in the aisle. When the buses were full, they lumbered down the country roads. At the sight of the departing buses, those lining the wall stood up and broke into a final song: "God Be with You 'til We

Meet Again." The bus was filled with the sound of weeping as the passengers turned towards those remaining to wave a final good-bye.

Hot tears stung Letta's eyes. She adjusted her body in order to see the prisoners singing. It seemed ironic that this was the song that had sent her on her original journey to China. Now this same song was being sung as she was leaving China. She shifted herself back around in her seat to stare blankly at the road stretching out in front of her. The sight of those prisoners singing their hearts out was so sad it was almost incomprehensible; one moment she was a prisoner just like them, and now she was free. It was all so overwhelming.

The buses rumbled past fields and the city suburbs to the train station. Once at the station, the prisoners were directed into the train station. The mid-day sun burned into their skin as they waited more than an hour for the train to arrive.

Letta was relieved to see the train from Tsingtao finally pull into the station. The 289 prisoners with their hand luggage were crammed into the third-class cars of the train. The soldiers kept pushing the prisoners into the trains until they were packed tightly like sardines.

There were no berths in the train compartments, only chairs or benches. The people outnumbered the seats. The passengers who couldn't find seats sat down in the aisles. Other passengers scrambled over each other looking for a place to rest in the already overcrowded baggage racks.

Letta and Harold tried to find seats, but their physical disabilities hindered them from moving fast enough. They managed to find a place in the aisle where the five of them could sit together. Harold's body creaked and strained as he attempted to squeeze his huge frame down onto the floor. Letta shifted some coats around, trying to make the floor as comfortable as possible for her dear husband. When she was sure that her family was settled in, she leaned against Harold and attempted to rest. No sooner had she fallen asleep, than the train stopped and jolted her awake.

Soldiers strode alongside the train compartments shouting out orders for the prisoners to disembark. Blurry-eyed and confused, people staggered up from where they were resting. Beads of perspiration glistened on their foreheads, and their throats were as dry as sandpaper.

Gwen pushed herself to her feet and tossed some bags into Margie's and Bud's hands. She bent over to help her parents stand up. The prisoners were herded off the train. They were told to wait while the cars of the train were transferred to a southbound train. While they were waiting on the platform a kindly Japanese officer allowed them to cross the tracks to a platform nearby. Water flowed freely from the pipes on that platform and everyone was able to be refreshed.

As evening drew near they moved back into the compartments and started off on their southbound journey. At midnight they arrived at Ping-P'u station. An order was given that the train would not leave the station until early the next morning. The air in the railroad cars was oppressively hot. After some talking with the guards, they allowed the men to sleep on the platform of the train station.

Early the next morning the overloaded train continued on its journey. Towards the latter part of the day the train reached Pukow station where all the prisoners disembarked and headed over to the ferry on the Yang-Tse River. Walking over to the ferry was no easy task. Letta and her family stumbled along the path in the drizzling rain. They strained under the heavy weight of their luggage. Some of the heavier luggage was carried by a group of forty stronger men. They had to make several trips back and forth before the final bag was piled on the ferry.

The ferry looked as though it would capsize under the weight of all the people and baggage. A man operating the ferry ran down to give last minute instructions on what to do if an emergency occurred once they were underway. His instructions brought little comfort to those squeezed on the ferry. Despite the overloading of the vessel, the trip crossing proved uneventful.

Once on the other side, everyone piled out onto the dock and headed off to the station. Again they were burdened with heavy bags. They trudged wearily through the rain towards the railroad station. Letta leaned on Gwen as she stumbled towards the station. No matter how hard she tried she couldn't move very fast. A guard prodded a bayonet into Letta's back.

He yelled at her, "Hurry up! Hurry Up! Get moving! Get moving!"

Harold looked over at his wife and wished he had the strength to pick her up, but he too was finding it difficult just to keep up.

They were greeted with bread and tea when they arrived at the Nanking railroad station. The soldiers pulled a cord across the platform to stop the prisoners from mingling with the other passengers. An announcement was made informing the prisoners that they would be required to wait for quite some time before they resumed their journey. Everyone constantly shifted positions, trying to get comfortable while they endured the long wait. Some had dozed off when the announcement was made that they were to board their next train.

Although the compartments proved to be overcrowded, at least they were bringing the prisoners closer to freedom. As the train journeyed towards Shanghai, the weather became unbearably hot. Thirst overwhelmed most of the prisoners. The train had only traveled a short time before it stopped again.

For three days the Hansens were pushed and shoved on and off trains. During the three-day journey, the prisoners were fed dry bread and tea twice. The journey normally would have taken only one and one-half days. The reason it took so long was because the Chinese were continually blowing up the tracks ahead of the train, but thankfully they never blew up the tracks close enough to harm the freed prisoners. The message they seemed to be sending to the Japanese army was that they were still not defeated.

They were saying, "You cannot do what you want; we are still in charge!" In the same way, they were sending a message to the prisoners that they should let the outside world know that the Chinese were putting up a strong resistance.

No one on the trains knew when they would reach their destination. They couldn't even be sure of where they were really being taken. They arrived at the Shanghai North station at noon and were told to get off the train and move towards the exit.

Stumbling through the station, the children held tight to the luggage as their parents moved slowly beside them. The guards were prodding them as usual with their bayonets, trying to force them to pick up their pace. Try as they could, Letta could not make herself walk any faster than she was already walking.

Slipping out the main exit of the station, they paused for a short while to catch their breath. No sooner had they started moving again away from the station when a hand grenade was hurled at the station, blowing it to bits.

The shock of the blast threw all of them off balance. Letta grabbed for her children and gathered them under her arms. She knew they could have easily been inside the station when it blew up! They had been walking so slowly, the blast could have killed all of them. Once again the Lord had sent His angels to camp around them and deliver them out of trouble. Whatever would happen on the rest of the journey, she knew God would go before them and continue to be with them. Almighty God was in control.

10

After leaving the Shanghai train station, the freed prisoners were subjected to yet another inspection. The Japanese soldiers rechecked their paperwork and rummaged through their luggage. They stood for hours as the Japanese soldiers searched through everyone's belongings. When they had combed through the Hansen's meager belongings, the soldiers stuffed a piece of paper into Rev. Hansen's hands. A frown spread across his brow as he read through the pamphlet written in choppy English. It was the list of regulations for the prisoners who were going to be embarking on the *Teia Maru*, the Japanese exchange ship.

Letta took the paper from Harold and read:

COMMANDER OF THE PRISONER ESCORT

NAVY OF THE JAPANESE EMPIRE

REGULATIONS FOR PRISONERS

1. The prisoners disobeying the following orders will be punished with immediate death.
   a.   Those disobeying orders and instructions
   b.   Those showing a motion of antagonism and raising signs of opposition

    c.   Those disobeying the regulations by individualism, egoism, thinking only about yourself, rushing for your own goods

    d.   Those talking without permission and raising loud voices

    e.   Those walking and moving without order

    f.   Those carrying unnecessary baggage in embarking

    g.   Those touching the boat's materials, wires, electric lights

    h.   Those climbing ladder without order

    i.   Those showing action or running away from the room or boat

    j.   Those trying to take more meal than given to them

    k.   Those using more than two blankets

2. Since the boat is not well equipped and inside being narrow, food being scarce and poor, you'll feel uncomfortable during the short time on the boat. Those losing patience and disordering the regulation will be heavily punished for the reason of not being able to escort.

3. Be sure to finish your nature's call evacuate the bowels and urine before embarking.

4. Meal will be given twice a day. One plate only to one prisoner. The prisoners called by the guard will give out the meal quick as possible and honestly. The remaining prisoners will stay in their places quietly and wait for your plate. Those moving from their places reaching for your plates without order will be heavily punished. Same orders will be applied in handling plates after meals.

5. Toilets will be fixed at the four corners of the sleeping area. The buckets and cans will be placed. When filled up a guard will appoint a prisoner. The prisoner called will take the buckets to the center of the room. The buckets will be pulled up by the derrick and be thrown away. Toilet papers will be given. Everyone must cooperate to make the room sanitary. Those being careless will be punished.

6. Navy of the Great Japanese Empire will not try to punish you all with death. Those obeying all the rules and regulations and believing the action and purpose of the Japanese Navy, cooperating with Japan in constructing the "New Order of the Great Asia" which lend to the world's peace will be well treated.

Letta handed the paper back to her husband. They stood restlessly waiting for the guards to finish the tiresome search.

After the examination everyone was assigned a makeshift dormitory room in an abandoned warehouse. They gulped down tea that was passed around and then moved to their assigned places. Simple folding canvas cots lined the floor. These cots looked wonderful after the three days of train travel they had just endured. Too exhausted to even bother with changing clothes, they flopped down onto their respective cots and fell fast asleep.

Sunday morning dawned with the hope of new beginnings. After a hurried breakfast of tea and bread, their hand luggage was examined again. Another roll call was given and everyone piled on buses so that they could be taken to the Customs House. Half the day was spent in the Customs House undergoing yet another tiresome inspection. After what seemed like an eternity the Hansens were herded out onto the jetty in front of the Customs House.

They could see the *Teia Maru*, an exchange ship waiting to carry them on the first part of their journey home. Glistening on the hull of the ship was a large white cross. And the Chinese characters for *Teia Maru* translated roughly to mean "ruling Asia" or "Imperial Asia."

The vessel was actually a French mail ship that had been converted into a ship to transport prisoners of war for the purpose of exchange. It would take them to Goa, India where they would be exchanged with over one thousand Japanese citizens who had been in the United States when the war broke out.

The total number of prisoners to fill up the steamer was 1,223. There were not enough life jackets or lifeboats because the steamer had only been equipped to handle 700 people.

Letta gazed out at the dilapidated vessel with a great deal of uncertainty.

The Teia Maru

She wondered at how this tired, old ship would be able to make the journey across the Indian Ocean, one of the worst of the three large oceans used for travel. There was no point wondering or questioning, because Letta had no choice in the matter; within a short time she would be loaded with her family onto a launch to go out to the *Teia Maru*. As always, she thanked God that He was in control of her life and that no matter what happened He had the best in mind for her and her family.

Once onboard, Letta and the girls were shoved towards the deck area. She looked around frantically for Harold and Bud, but soon realized they had been herded in a different direction. Women with small babies were pushed along towards the cabin area. They were assigned long, narrow cabins to share. The soldiers moved the rest of the females along the outside of the decks and handed them straw pallets. Apparently they were expected to lay their pallets down right on the decks.

Letta still felt a bit disorientated being separated from Harold. All through their internment, no matterhow bad things had gotten, they had been allowed to stay together. Letta and Gwen worked together to set up their sleeping area. With limited space, they had to overlap the mats so that they could fit the three pallets together. Using their clothing and some string, Letta created a makeshift curtain around the mats. The improvised curtains were their only means of retaining some element of privacy. This would be their 'home' for the next month.

The majority of the male prisoners were pushed towards the gaping hole that led down to the hold. This black abyss was the place where huge crates were usually stored. Harold and Bud carefully made their way down the steep stairs leading down into the hold. The lower they went the more oppressive the heat became. Harold found great difficulty in navigating the steep stairs due to his crippled knees. Bud dropped the straw mats he had been lugging and flopped down on the grimy floor. Harold grimaced as he maneuvered his body down beside his son. The stench of the hold invaded their nostrils, causing them to gag. They had no idea how they were going to spend weeks in this God-forsaken place. They were literally in the bowels of the steamer.

The first few days aboard the *Teia Maru* were spent adjusting to the new surroundings.

Everything felt oily and grimy. The steamer looked as though it would fall apart at any moment. Letta tried to block out the general disarray and concentrated on cleaning up their little corner of the ship to make it feel as comfortable as possible. She was relieved to discover that apart from meal times and sleeping times, Harold and Bud were allowed to meet up with the rest of the family on the decks.

The food onboard was far better than what they had ever eaten in the concentration camp, But there simply was not enough food to satisfy their ongoing hunger. The prisoners always felt as though only about sixty percent of their hunger was actually satisfied. Much of the food was hoarded by the Japanese guards and later sold on the decks. Prisoners traded valuable items for food.

The women and men were separated when the food was distributed. The men were forced to eat down in the hold of the ship. When Harold saw that they were getting rice he was very happy. While in the concentration camp they had only eaten bread, and he longed for rice. Prisoners who had come from other camps were not as thrilled, since they had existed only on rice throughout their internment.

Bud looked at his rice and turned to his dad commenting, "Dad, the rice is full of worms!"

Harold chomped away on his ration and replied, "Bud, Dr. Brown told me that those worms are full of vitamins. They have been living on nothing but the good rice."

The worms didn't stop Harold from eating up his full portion of rice and then asking the prisoners next to him for their portions. They couldn't stand the sight of the worms, but he consoled himself with the fact that the worms were rather healthy, as they had been feeding on nothing but rice.

The women fared slightly better than the men. They were given some sweet desserts after their rice meal. Sometimes they would get a little sponge cake that tasted delicious. The men didn't receive any sweets because the soldiers sold them on the black market.

The soldiers distributed the water for one hour in the morning and one hour in the evening. During that time of water distribution the prisoners had to collect as much water as they needed for the rest of the day. What a mad scramble there was as 1,223 prisoners fell over each other trying to get their much-needed supply of water.

Aside from the food and water rationing, the prisoners worried about their safety. At one point the steamer passed through waters that were riddled with mines. A pilot ship took the steamer through the dangerous area. While the steamer maneuvered its way through the hazardous waters, those on board battled with fear. They realized that one little mistake could cost them their lives! The Christians set their hope in the Lord, realizing their safety was in the hands of God. Those who hadn't put their trust in the Lord experienced terrible times of fear and consternation.

The difficulties they faced on the steamer could not compare with what they had been through in the concentration camp. In fact, Letta kept thanking God every day for the way He had delivered them from the trials and tribulations of the camp.

As the ship sailed down the coast of China, the weather proved to be warm and the waters calm. Within a couple days they had reached the waters of Hong Kong where the ship anchored in Stanley Bay.

There was no proper communication given as to why they were there, so the prisoners just walked around the decks looking out towards the distant wharf. After a period of twenty-four hours they were greeted with a small group of repatriates from Hong Kong. Letta watched as they clambered onboard, looking around fearfully at those who were already there. Her heart went out to them and she made a point to go forward and welcome them aboard. A bit of shifting took place on the decks as the new arrivals squeezed into the already crowded living space.

The ship took off from Hong Kong and arrived in Philippine waters on a Sunday. This was the first Sunday to be celebrated onboard, and each of the Christians wanted to have a proper worship time. It was arranged that the Catholics would use one of the dining halls and the Anglicans would use another hall. Their services were held in the morning. The rest of the Christians had a joint meeting in the evening in the first class dining hall. Letta felt so refreshed to be joining together to give thanks to God for bringing them safe thus far. After the service they stayed behind to discuss setting up Bible studies and other prayer meetings to be held throughout the week. It seemed as if life was moving more in the direction of normalcy, or rather, as normal as it could get at that point.

When the prisoners of war had approached the officers about holding Bible studies and prayer meetings, they had kindly agreed. The prisoners were given permission to use the second-class dining room each morning between 9:10 and 10:30. They rejoiced in the fact they had the privilege to meet together to sing songs of worship, to study the Word, and to pray. There were no hymnals, so they sang songs from memory. Mainly they sang songs such as, "Higher Ground," "Nearer, My God, to Thee," and "Jesus, Lover of My Soul." The presence of the Holy Spirit permeated the meetings from the start to the finish.

The young people met every morning to study the Bible and every evening to hold a song service. The faith of the young people was renewed, and they grew in leaps and bounds in their relationship with the Lord.

These times of refreshing were much—needed! Prior to the internment in the concentration camp, the Hansens had enjoyed wonderful outpourings of the Holy Spirit in Peking. Once they went to the intern- ment camp it seemed that God's work had come to a standstill. They worked so hard in the camp just to survive. All their strength was focused on survival, barely leaving time to pray. The longing in their hearts could not be contained! In the last prayer meeting they attended at the camp, practically every testimony told of the great longing for a special outpouring of the Holy Spirit. Now on the steamer, the Lord was granting the desires of their hearts. He sent such a powerful outpouring of the Holy Spirit. Their hearts were hardly able to contain the wonders of His might and power! Before the ship left the Philippines a group of one hundred and thirty repatriates came on board. Those on the ship couldn't wait for these new arrivals to get onboard so they could ply them with questions. They hoped they might have more recent news of what was going on in the war.

Once the new prisoners were onboard, the repatriates from China quickly welcomed them and set them up in their new living arrangements. Inevitably, they were quizzed as to the conditions of the concentration camps they had just been in. Letta was saddened when she heard of the terrible conditions of the other camps, but it made her realize that Camp Wei Hsein had been one of the better camps. There hadn't been as many casualties, there hadn't been as many deaths, and the cruelty didn't seem to be as bad as what she was hearing about other camps.

The next stop on their journey was the port of Saigon. More prisoners were picked up, mostly missionaries, as well as some meat, vegetables, and fruits. These foodstuffs were not for the prisoners but were to be taken to another port.

The anchor was drawn and Letta stood holding onto the railing as the ship moved lazily down the Mekong River. If she didn't turn around and look at the makeshift bedding lined up behind her, she could almost believe that she was on a luxurious voyage. She drew her breath as she looked out at the jungles lining the side of the river and the birds flitting in and out of the trees. It wasn't long before the ship moved back out into the open sea. Letta sighed and turned away from the railing to go back to her resting area. It wasn't long before they anchored in Singapore and picked up more prisoners there. When the ship left Singapore it took a rather roundabout route to get to India. When some of the prisoners tried to ask the guards why this route had been taken, they brushed them aside. It was generally believed that this route was being made to avoid a mined area in the sea west of Singapore.

On October 15th the *Teia Maru* sliced through the waters near Goa, India. Letta and her family stood on the deck looking out towards the dock. For ten days they had seen nothing but water, so it was wonderful to allow their eyes to feast on the scenery that lay before them. At most of the other ports they were anchored out at sea, but here they were being taken right up to the docks.

As they pulled up alongside the wharf and the sailors moved quickly to throw strong wire cables alongside the ship to harness it, a gangplank was lowered and some guards positioned themselves at the top and the bottom of the gangplank.

Letta could feel her heart pounding in her chest. She had been told that this was where they would be transferred to the *M.S. Gripsholm*, the ship repatriating them to American soil. Her mind was finding it hard to digest this new series of events.

"Mama! Look! They're using cranes to unload our luggage!" shouted Bud.

The cranes moved systematically unloading all the pieces of heavy luggage that had been stored in the ship's hold. Letta leaned over the side of the ship to see what would become of the luggage. As soon as it hit the ground it was picked up by some Indian porters and transported to a nearby warehouse where it would be stacked alphabetically.

Excitement filled the air. The passengers milled about aimlessly, eagerly awaiting further instructions. It wasn't long before they were divided alphabeti- cally and given instructions to go ashore to unpack and repack their trunks.

Stepping off the gangplank onto the shore felt wonderful. After a brief period of unpacking and repacking, they returned to the ship. The following morning, much to Letta's delight, they were allowed to go on shore once again. A small area was set aside for the prisoners to enjoy stretching their legs. It wasn't long after Letta had gotten off the ship that she was stopped in her tracks by the sight of a huge vessel approaching the wharf. Lifting up her hands to shield her eyes, Letta tried to get a better look at the majestic vessel. The deck of the *M.S. Gripsholm* stood high above all the other ocean liners along the wharf. Tears pricked at the corners of Letta's eyes as she viewed the grand ship that would carry her family to freedom. Glancing over at Harold, she could see that the sight of the ship had overwhelmed him as well. The passengers on the dock were then quickly ushered back onboard the *Teia Maru* to await their final disembarkation (since they were still considered prisoners and had to be accounted for at every moment).

Letta pulled down the makeshift curtain around their mats. Gwen and Margaret bundled the clothes together and waited patiently for Harold and Bud to join them on the upper deck.

Letta found herself smiling spontaneously for the first time in a very long while. After spending a month on the *Teia Maru*, she had regained more strength. The children chattered away with their friends, and everyone was excited knowing they would soon be leaving the ship.

None of them knew what lay ahead of them, but they were hoping it would be somewhat better than what they had been through during the past month.

The process of transferring the prisoners was systematically organized. The passengers stood by their sleeping quarters awaiting specific instructions for the exchange. Some guides went up and down the rows of passengers and led them to the appropriate place for disembarkation. The guards set up the exchange in such a way that the prisoners from the Japanese steamer went down one way and those from the American ship entered via another way. They didn't want the two sets of prisoners to have any contact with one another.

As the Hansens came up onto the deck of the *M.S. Gripsholm*, they took a deep breath. They smelled the scent of freedom as they boarded this American controlled liner. There still would be some strict conditions on this vessel, but instinctively they knew it would be better than the conditions they had endured over the past few months.

Letta couldn't get over the fact that everything looked so different on this ship. They had come from grime and dirt and a vessel practically falling apart, and now they were on a vessel that rose up in majesty and splendor.

Margaret grabbed Letta's arm and gasped, "Mama, Look!!"

There in front of the Hansens were tables full of food stretched out the full length of the deck of the ship. Every table looked like a Swedish smorgas-bord. All types of delicacies, meats, and vegetables filled the tables! Letta squeezed her eyes shut and then opened them again; the food was still there. This was not a dream.

The passengers gaped at the delicious food spread out before them. They turned and looked at each other in disbelief. Tears streamed down the cheeks of all the prisoners, and even the most cynical of the passengers began weeping openly at the sight of the sumptuous food. Everyone spontaneously turned to whoever was standing next to them and hugged with joy.

Red Cross workers moved noiselessly amongst the passengers distributing clothing, blankets, and shoes. Letta stood with her arms filled with more than she thought she could hold. Someone else would walk by and deposit a sweater or a chocolate bar on top of her ever-growing mound of goodies. Tears flowed like streams down her cheeks. She turned to look at the other prisoners and saw that she was not the only one crying.

Someone was overheard whispering loudly, "If there is a heaven on earth this must surely be it!"

The *M.S. Gripsholm* had been built in 1925 as a luxurious ocean liner. Many people had traveled on the Gripsholm enjoying fabulous holidays in South America and Europe. The vessel was built with elegance, and everything about it spoke of beauty. In 1942 the ship had been commandeered by the United States government to help in the repatriation of their nationals from enemy territory. For those who had come out of the concentration camps across Asia, this ship was indeed a bit of heaven on earth!

It didn't take long for the Hansens to be ushered to their living quarters. Letta walked into both the spacious cabins and shed more tears of joy. She

The M.S. Gripsholm

deposited her load on the bed of her cabin and walked slowly around the room touching every fixture and furnishing. It was as if she had to feel the items in the room to convince herself this was not a dream.

She wandered through the ship soaking up the beauty around her. She opened a door that led into the Rose Room, which was decorated tastefully in various hues of rose. Her eyes drank up the matching carpet, the lounge chairs, the lamps and the shades. She had been so thirsty for beauty, and now she was able to quench that thirst. Each room she ventured in looked more beautiful than the room she had left. Her heart rose up with such thankfulness to God for preserving her family and for bringing them through the hard times. She gave thanks to Him for allowing them the wonderful blessing of traveling back home on this luxurious ship!

They had boarded the Gripsholm on the 19th of October, and remained in port until Thursday, October 21, 1943. Bud was the first one to announce that the ship was preparing to depart; as he had seen the crew busy with loosening the cables and getting the anchor pulled up. Letta went up on deck to watch as they pulled away from the dock. At first she was looking down towards the dock itself, but then the sound of singing drifted towards her. She moved towards the stern where the sound was coming from. She saw the Japanese prisoners lining the stern of their ship as it pulled away. Those on the *M.S. Gripsholm* were singing "God Be with You 'Til We Meet Again" and the Japanese on the *Teia Maru* were responding with the same song. The Japanese officers tried to stop the singing but they could not make them stop. The prisoners on both vessels waved to each other.

As soon as the Gripsholm was underway, the mail distribution began. Letta was in her room when Harold brought her the letters from home. She looked at each envelope carefully.

"Mama, open them up!" Margie urged excitedly. "Be patient, Margie. I will open it up but there is no need to rush." Letta responded.

Letta read through several letters smiling at the news of her family back home. She tore open a final letter only to find that it contained sad news. Her mother had fallen down and broken her hip. Letta put the letter back down on her lap and turned towards the porthole. She swallowed the lump in her throat and picked the letter back up to finish reading it. How she wished she could be with her mother helping her at this difficult time. If only the journey would go by quickly so that she could get home to help her mother. She realized she was now in great need of the patience that she had so easily required of Margie.

Comfort was easy to get used to. It didn't take long for the passengers to fall into a nice routine onboard. The Christians asked the officers onboard the ship if they would be allowed to meet each day for services.

Their request was granted, and the meetings that had begun on the Japanese steamer continued on the *M.S. Gripsholm*.

One day while they had gathered for a meeting on the deck of the Gripsholm, the rain pelted down on the group. They prayed and asked the Lord to turn the rain away, and immediately the prayer was answered. The sun shone brightly and became a testimony to those who were just standing nearby listening to what was going on.

One thing that was hard for the passengers to fully comprehend was the fact that they had gained freedom from the moment they boarded the *M.S. Gripsholm*. It was not until they arrived at their first port, Port Elizabeth, South Africa, that the passengers truly understood they were no longer prisoners. They were told they could disembark and go shopping or sightseeing. How exciting to know that they had the freedom to decide whether they wanted to remain on board or get off the ship. At any port where they docked, the passengers were allowed to disembark and roam about freely.

When the ship docked in Rio de Janeiro, Letta wanted to disembark with the other passengers. The sights and sounds were wonderful. She went along with a group of passengers who were going to the marketplace. As she walked through the makeshift stalls, she kept looking for something in particular. Finally she found what she was looking for, a delicate serving tray. The tray was decorated with gorgeous, iridescent South American butterflies on a layer of cotton. The beautiful setting was held tightly in place with a glass covering.

Later back onboard the ship, Letta gingerly unwrapped the tray and held it up to admire it. Margie couldn't take her eyes off the tray.

Touching the tray gingerly she asked, "What did you buy this tray for, Mama?"

Letta kept her eyes fastened on the tray and smiled.

"Honey, grandma is very ill. She is so ill she can't get out of bed. I thought to myself, wouldn't it be nice to cheer her up by serving her breakfast in bed on a beautiful tray like this."

Letta carefully wrapped up the tray and tucked it deep into her bag. Once again she felt the deep longing to be reunited with her family and to make sure that her mother recovered. It saddened her heart that she wasn't able to be right there with her mother taking care of her as she had so often taken care of Letta in the past.

The Hansens spent a full forty-three days on the *M.S.Gripsholm*. God used their time onboard to bring about the beginning of healing from the pain and hardship they had suffered. They could feel their bodies relax and unwind from the months of tension they had lived through.

On, December 1, 1943, the *M.S. Gripsholm* docked in the New York harbor. Wild cheers erupted from the passengers when they spotted Lady Liberty in the harbor; they couldn't believe they were actually home!

Standing up on the deck each passenger experienced a kaleidoscope of emotions. So much had transpired between the time they left their various internment camps and arrived safely back in the United States. There had been times when they doubted if they'd ever make it, and yet here they were, by the grace of God.

When they were given the final instruction for disembarkation, the Hansens rushed back down to their cabin to gather up their meager belongings. Letta packed up the few cases they had and went through the cabin one last time to double check that nothing was left behind. Looking around the cabin, she thanked God for the restoration He had brought to their souls while they were on this vessel. Once she was sure that everything was in order, she told the children to sit down for one last time of devotions on the ship.

"Children, let me give you a verse before we get off this ship," Letta said, "I want you to leave this ship with this verse in mind. Let's turn to Isaiah 55:12:

For ye shall go out with joy and be led forth with peace. The Mountains and the hills will break forth into shouts of joy before you, and all the trees of the field will clap their hands.

Let us leave this ship with joy and let us go forth with peace! We have so much to be thankful for."

The Red Cross roamed the deck of the *M.S. Gripsholm* welcoming the passengers back home. Letta grasped her large Hershey chocolate bar and thick wool sweater. Everyone on board was being given the same gifts. Letta stopped on the deck and looked out across the crowded dock. Her eyes glistened with unshed tears of joy as she soaked in the beauty of her homeland. Her children squeezed around her all talking excitedly at once, their happy exclamations gushing out like a cheerful waterfall. Letta lifted her eyes to heaven and thanked God for preserving her family. She knew that her journey in life had not come to an end, but now more than ever she had an assurance that God would direct her path.

11

Final clearance was given to disembark, and the Hansens were instructed to go to the shipping offices to pick up an important message that had come in for them. They jostled through the crowded dock navigating their way to the office. The pace they were able to keep was much faster than just a few months earlier when they had left Camp Wei Hsein. The time spent on the *M.S. Gripsholm* had allowed for physical rest and healing to take place.

After weaving in and out of the crowd, the Hansens reached a small office.

"Excuse me, sir," Letta politely called to the man sitting in the small shipping office. It didn't take long for her to explain to the man why she was there. He found her message and slid it across the counter asking her to sign the receipt for it. After signing for the message, she tore it open with trembling hands and scanned the contents. Her face paled and she caught her breath. Slowly Letta raised her eyes and looked back at Harold in shock.

"What's wrong, Letta?" Harold asked, instinctively moving closer to her.

Letta's eyes glazed over as she responded, "It's Mama. She is gone, Harold. She went to be with Jesus on Nov. 18th while we were still at sea. There is no need to hurry now; we should just wait for Andy so we can travel together to Washington to be with Daddy and the rest of the family."

"Oh, honey, I'm so sorry." Harold reached over and touched his wife's shoulder offering her consolation.

Still staring straight ahead she whispered, "It's okay; she is with Jesus. That is all that really matters."

Letta glanced over at the children and smiled weakly, and then she reached down to pick up her suitcase and marched out of the small office. She never let on to anyone the pain and disappointment she had inside. She had too much to do and too many things to settle; she couldn't dwell on the loss of her beloved mother.

A distant ache lingered with her over the next few days as they settled down in a missionary guesthouse in New York. Adjusting back to life in America took every bit of strength and energy. How does one adjust to being free? No one told you where you needed to sleep that night or which dining hall you were expected to eat in. It had been many long months since they'd had the privilege of making all their own decisions.

The children didn't think about the decisions that had to be made. They were just happy to be free to enjoy life in the natural exuberance of youth. They eagerly explored the sights and went up the Empire State Building. The time in the internment camp and on the exchange ships quickly became a distant memory that thankfully was now clouded out with all their fun activities.

The days were easy to get through because they were so full of things to do, but nights were the hardest for Letta. When the last child was safely tucked in bed, she faced a private battle with her memories of her mother. She had to fight through the disappointment and the hurt she felt over her mother's death.

On one particular night Letta was still sitting on the edge of Margie's bed after getting her daughter to settle down into sleep; she sat listening to the hum of street noises outside the window when she had a sudden thought. On impulse, Letta leaned forward and fumbled through her suitcase that for some reason was still sitting in the corner of Margie's room. Her hands located the tray she had bought in Rio de Janeiro. She set the package on her lap and stared at it. Her fingers gingerly untied the string that held the package together. She pulled back the layers of wrapping around the tray, and as she removed each layer she felt as though she was peeling back the layers that had been shielding her from her pain. Finally the last layer was off and the tray lay in her lap. A tear slipped down her cheek as she traced the outline of the beautiful butterflies on the tray. That one tear unleashed a flood of sobs gushing out from deep within her soul. Margie woke up to the sounds of her mother's sobs. Sleepily rubbing her eyes, she asked, "What's the matter, Mama? Why are you crying?"

Letta had tried to be strong in front of her children, but the pain was overwhelming. She patted Margie's head and explained to her why she was so torn apart.

"I wanted to be with my mother and take care of her, Margie. Do you remember how I told you I bought this beautiful tray so that I could serve her in bed? Oh honey, you can't imagine how my heart broke when I heard that my mother had gone to heaven before I could see her one last time."

Margie lay there looking up at her mother's tear-stained cheeks. In all that her mother had been through, she had not seen her cry this way. Her mama was such a brave woman. She was the one always listening to other people's problems and never burdening them with her own problems. She never complained or felt sorry for herself. Every day she kept her pain inside so that her family wouldn't be burdened with her loss. Margie now understood a bit of the disappointment and pain her mother had to bear. She admired her mother for her courage and strength to keep going on. In her young girl's heart Margie knew that somehow, eventually, that tray would no longer represent sadness, but instead would bring sweet memories to comfort her mother.

Letta wasn't one to dwell on things that couldn't be changed. The time to leave on the journey west came very quickly. She knew she couldn't keep looking behind, but instead had to look forward to what lie ahead. The morning dawned for their departure; Letta was up early organizing everyone for the long journey to Springfield, Missouri.

The train chugged out of the New York station heading west. Letta couldn't help but notice the difference of this train trip compared with the trips she had been on a few months earlier. The previous trips had been overshadowed by anxiety and fear, but this trip caused hope to well up inside.

When they arrived in Springfield, the Hansens went directly to the Assemblies of God headquarters to meet with the leaders. They were requested to give a full report to the officials there of all that they had been through and of any information they had concerning missionaries who still remained in China. Prayers of thanksgiving were offered up for their safe return from China.

After a whirlwind of activity, the Hansens continued on the next leg of the journey to California where they visited with Harold's family. Each part of the journey brought a different level of much-needed healing.

The final part of their journey took them to Tacoma, Washington. Twenty-three years from the time Letta first left Washington for China, she was now back to stay. Things had changed, not just in the city but also in Letta's heart. She had grown stronger and had learned what it really meant to trust in God with her whole heart.

To usher in the new year of 1944, the Hansen family went together to the Tacoma First Assembly of God. . This was the church that had so faithfully supported Letta when she first went to China. What a joy to be back together with these faithful congregants to look forward to the New Year and what God would do in it.

Andrew Teuber, or Uncle Andy as the children affectionately called him, was the pastor of the Assemblies of God church in Omak, Washington. He couldn't begin to fathom all that his sister and her family had been through, and he wanted to help in some way. He took Harold and Letta aside and questioned them about what they planned to do. They responded that they were just going to trust the Lord. They had nothing that belonged to them; their only hope was in the Lord.

Uncle Andy had been building a house for their parents, but now that their mother had died, he suggested that Letta and her family move in to the house when it was complete to take care of their father and Letta's younger sister Elta Teuber.

"While we are waiting for the house to be completed, I will rent a small

Tribune

RLD . . . UNITED PRESS

RATIONING TIM

MEAT, CANNED FISH, BUTTER, COOKING OIL
October 30.
SUGAR—Stamp 14, Book 1, five pounds through
through October 31.
PROCESSED FRUITS AND VEGETABLES—Blue
Blue X, Y, Z, through November 20.
SHOES—Stamp 18, Book 1, indefinite; "Airplane"
1, 1944.
GASOLINE—A coupon 8, three gallons, through N
TIRE INSPECTIONS—A tires, March 31; B tires,

FRIDAY, OCT. 15, 1943·   1

Berkeley will be very welcome to Mr. and Mrs. Harold E. Hansen and their three children, who are coming home on the Gripsholm after a life-time of missionary work in the Orient and a siege in a Jap concentration camp. This picture, taken several years ago, shows Harold, now 15, Hansen, Gwendolyn, now 18, and Margaret, 12.

house for you near the school," Andy explained.

"You are being so good to us!" Letta exclaimed. It didn't take long for the house to be completed.

On the morning of moving day, Andy drove over to help them get their things packed up. There weren't a lot of things so the moving process was easy.

The car moved slowly up the side of the hill until it reached the house perched on the top of the hill. Letta stepped out of the car and breathed in

Hansen family

the country air. From where she stood she could see out over a small valley. Turning towards the large house, she saw a sprawling yard with trees, and she just couldn't believe that this was her new home. Spinning around, she threw her arms around Andy's neck and hugged him with all her strength, thanking her brother over and over. There didn't seem to be enough words to express the joy she felt at that moment, but then she thought of one: home. They had finally come home. God provided another opportunity for healing.

The house was big enough for the Hansens and for Letta's father and her dear sister Elta. Gwen and Margie shared a room with Elta down in the basement, and Bud occupied another room in the basement. Letta and Harold moved into rooms upstairs. Letta's father also had a room upstairs.

Letta settled right in taking care of her father, her husband, and her younger sister. Her father being older in years needed a lot of tender loving care. Letta was more than happy to give him all the care that he needed. She had missed out on so many years of caring for her father, and she treasured this time that she could spend with him. Harold still was very weak from his ordeal in China and he also needed a lot of care. Elta had epilepsy so she also needed Letta to look after her.

The children were growing up right before Letta's eyes. Gwen had already completed high school while they were on the *M.S. Gripsholm*, so she was preparing to go to Bible College in Southern California. Bud and Margie went to the nearby high school. When Letta wasn't busy with her family or church work, she found the garden to be a special place of rest. She planted a beautiful garden and raised vegetables, and through this garden God continued to work a deep healing within her.

The family attended the Omak church where Andy Teuber was the pastor. Many of Letta's relatives lived in the surrounding area so she enjoyed the fellowship of her family. Her sister Faith and her husband were in Chelan, Washington. Her other sister Edith and her husband were the pastors of the Assemblies of God church in Wenatchee.

During their time in Omak, Harold and Letta were active in the church. They were faithful in witnessing and counseling. Whenever there was a need in the church they were the first to offer their help. But despite their willingness to minister to others, somehow both Letta and Harold understood that their time in Omak was also a time for them to be ministered to. They needed this time to recuperate and rest after all they had endured in the concentration camp.

The time came for Gwen to leave for Southern California Bible College in Pasadena, California. Letta helped her pack her little suitcase. They had spent so much time together in the past two years; it was difficult to imagine being separated. As they got everything ready for Gwen's departure, Letta would steal a look at her daughter. She had grown up into a fine young lady with a desire to put God first in her life. The difficult time during the war had taught Gwen more than Letta could have ever hoped to teach her. Now it was time for Letta to let her go to pursue what God had in store for her life.

Bud and Margie still needed a lot of attention. Bud was finishing up in high school, and Margie had just started high school. They were busy with church and their friends.

One day Margie stomped in from school and said, "I just want to inform you that I am never going back to church again, so don't try and make me go. I don't ever want to go to church; I'm not interested in it."

Letta stopped folding clothes and said, "Margie, why would you not want to go to church? Tell me what is wrong."

"Mama, you just won't believe what happened to me today," Margie blurted out.

"There was this girl in my class. She is with the Free Methodist Church. She came up to me in school today and said, 'By the way, how does it feel to be demon possessed?'"

"I was shocked that she said that to me, so I told her that I didn't think I was, and then I asked her why she thought I was demon-possessed. Oh Mama, by this time I was feeling half sick wondering why she would ever say such things about me."

Letta pulled Margie close to her and rubbed her shoulders, "Oh honey, I'm so sorry that happened to you. But what does that have to do with you not wanting to go to church?"

Margie continued on with her story. "The girl told me that a lady from our church who works on the apple sorting belt told some of the other women who work on the belt that I was demon-possessed. Oh, Mama!! Can you believe that? I am finished with church!"

Letta looked squarely at her daughter for a moment, and then she told her to sit down. She sat down next to her and held her hand.

"Margie, I want to ask you some questions," she said. "Has Jesus ever told you a lie?"

"No, Mama." Margie responded.

"Has Jesus ever cheated you, has He ever disappointed you, has He ever done anything wrong against you?" Letta continued.

Margie looked up at her mother and said, "No, Mama, of course not!"

"Has He ever done anything but love you?" Margie looked down at her hands and mumbled,

"No, Mama."

Letta put her finger under Margie's chin, lifting her face up so she could look right into her daughter's eyes, and then she said, "Then why would you want to leave Jesus?"

Margie fell into her mother's arms and broke down crying. "Oh, Mama, I'm sorry! You've always taught me that Jesus is more important than anyone else. My eyes got off Jesus and onto people."

Letta continued to hug Margie and let her cry away the hurt and the pain. Letta had always taught the children that Jesus was so precious and wonderful. From the time they were young she had made sure they got up early to spend time in family devotions. Even when she would ride around in the rickshaws in China, she pulled the children up on her lap and worked with them on scripture memorization. Now they were learning for themselves how special Jesus could be in their lives. She stood back to see the Word that she had been planting in their hearts all these years sprouting forth and bearing fruit in their lives.

In 1945, Bud went to join his sister Gwen at Southern California Bible College. He felt the call of God on his life, and he was eager to answer that call. It thrilled Letta to see her children following after the same call she had on her life.

With two children out of the nest, Letta now had more time to spend with her sister Elta. She treasured the time she had with Elta. Elta had only been 14 years old when Letta left for China, so now she found she had a wonderful opportunity to get to know her little sister. Elta would go door to door selling Bibles, and when she came home she would share with Letta the testimonies of how people came to know the Lord. Together they would rejoice over all the things that God continued to do in their lives.

The time soon came for Margie to decide what she was going to do after she graduated from high school. It disturbed Letta that Margie was not that keen about going to Bible School. She had gotten it into her head that she would be a journalist. Letta took the matter to the Lord in prayer and laid out the whole situation before Him. After praying over the matter, she took Margie aside and told her that she would prefer it if Margie spent one year in Bible School so that God would have a chance to speak to her heart.

"At least then you would give God a chance if He was calling you into ministry. You would be in the right place to hear Him. Now, if after a year you don't feel you have the call of God on your life, you can pick up something else. At least you will have given that year of your life to study the Word of God." Letta said.

Much to her relief, Margie decided to go to Bible School. In the same year that Margie went off to Bible school, Gwen went to China as a Junior Missionary to work with Rev. Paul Moransburg in Nanking. Letta couldn't contain her joy seeing her eldest daughter following in her footsteps and going back to the country that had rooted itself in her heart.

Now her contact with her three children was through letters. Every letter that came would be read carefully and prayed over fervently. Gwen's letters told of the ongoing changes that were taking place in China. She had to move down to Shanghai as the communists continued to push across China. Their advance didn't stop, and soon it was necessary for Gwen to go over to Formosa to continue her work with Rev. Paul Moransburg. After a two-year commitment, Gwen returned back to the States. She planned to stay for a short time and head back to Formosa, but when she was given her medical exam they discovered some problems that prohibited her from being sent back to the field. Gwen ran to Letta for reassurance, feeling devastated by the prospect of not being able to return to the mission field.

Letta encouraged Gwen by saying, "God knows what He is doing, Gwen. Our Lord knows exactly where you are supposed to be and when you are to be there. Let's just leave this in His hands now."

It didn't take long for Gwen to find out that God wanted her to go for a nurse's training course in Los Angeles. She knew there was more than one way to serve God, and she wanted to prepare herself for what He had in store for her.

Letta knew from experience that God always knew best. She had seen it in her own life, and she was seeing now in the lives of her children that God could step in and turn them in the right direction. She watched Margie quit Bible School after just one year there. The Dean of Women from the

Southern California Bible College approached her towards the end of the school year and told her not to come back the next year unless she knew she had a calling on her life from God. Letta knew Margie was called, but she also knew that until Margie understood that fact for herself there would be no point in convincing her to go back. There were things that needed to be settled in Margie's life before she could go back and fulfill the call on her life.

Letta found herself kneeling before the Lord and lifting up her family to him once again. He was always so faithful. He had guided her family throughout the years; surely He would not fail her now. She cherished the daily sessions she had at His feet unburdening her soul to Him. When she got up from her times alone with Him, she knew that all would be well. Anyone who lived with Letta knew not to disturb her when she was having her times with her Savior.

God worked in Margie's heart during her time back home. She settled herself in a job and a relationship with a nice young man. One night when she went to a meeting at the church in Omak, Rev. Fulton Buntain was sharing the message. As she sat there listening to Him speaking, she felt as though God was speaking directly to her, and she felt a strong call to the mission field to serve Him.

After the meeting Letta could see that Margie was disturbed. She chose not to say anything to her daughter, but instead just to pray for her to make the right decision. She didn't realize that Margie was struggling with the fact that if she were truly called then she would have to give up her relationship with her boyfriend. He didn't have the same calling on his life. Within two weeks from the time Margie knew she was called, God had the boy break off their relationship. Although she felt hurt by this rejection, she now knew that God had really called her, and so she prepared herself to go back to school.

Letta couldn't believe her ears when Margie told her she was going back to school. Her heart overflowed with thanks to the Lord for pointing her daughter in the right direction once again. When Margie mentioned to her the problem of finding money to pay for her school tuition, Letta assured her that if God had brought her this far, surely He would take care of her tuition.

Miraculously God allowed Margie to become known to a group that sponsored girls to college. When Margie was told about this group, she applied for the funds to go to back to Bible College. One day after the Sunday service, Margie went into the prayer room at the church. She began to petition God in regards to her request for the funding. After praying for some time she went home and found Letta in the kitchen at the stove.

"Mama, I'm going to be the girl who is chosen out of the whole state of Washington. I'm going to be chosen, but I don't understand because I applied for $600 — because that is how much it costs for a year — but in a vision I just had I only got $450. I don't understand that part of the vision, but I'm sure I'm going to be the one chosen!"

Letta hugged Margie and assured her that no matter what happened, she knew God would work things out. The very next day Margie received word that she had been chosen and they were sorry but the program had a limit of $450 per year, so the vision had been accurate. Once again God was faithful in His provision for her children.

Six years had passed since their arrival in Omak. The Lord had been good to them in their times of adjustment, healing, and restoration. Letta had been given a chance to watch her children blossom into adults, each having a heart after God's own heart. Now the time had come for Harold and Letta to get back into frontline ministry. They were asked to be the pastors of a church in Okanogan. They didn't waste any time making up their minds. They accepted the offer and took over the church. Although it had been many years since they were pastors of a church, they had not stopped being involved with ministry. The whole time they were in the Omak church they had kept very involved with ministry. They had no trouble adjusting to their new position as pastors of the church in Okanogan.

12

The year 1950 dawned with much hope and promise. God had been good to Letta and her family during the seven years since they returned from China. The horrors of their final years in China seemed like a faded bad dream. Letta's children were busy pursuing the call of God on their lives. She and her husband worked together to take care of their flock in the Okanogan church. Her father, although older in years, was still vibrant and excited about the Lord.

Evenings were the best time of the day for Letta. The household gathered around the dinner table to eat and exchange testimonies of God's goodness. Elta always had something to share about her days spent witnessing and selling Bibles. Letta often found herself lingering around the table enjoying the warmth of her family.

After one such pleasant evening, Elta stood up to help Letta clear off the table. They fell into their normal routine of washing dishes together, continuing their chatter at the sink. No matter how much they talked to each other, there always seemed to be more that needed to be said. Letta loved the way her sister put God first in everything she did and said.

Once the last dish had been wiped, Elta turned to Letta and asked, "Are there anymore dishes for me to do or anything else you need me to do?"

Letta reached up and pushed a stray bit of hair back off her forehead.

She half turned to face Elta and responded, "I can't think of anything now. Anyways there is always tomorrow."

Elta folded the dishcloth neatly and laid it on the counter next to Letta.

"You might not see me tomorrow." She said softly.

Letta swung around to face her sister. She tilted her head to the side and furrowed her brow as she studied her sister's face. A sweet smile played at the corner of Elta's lips as she leaned forward to brush Letta's cheek with a goodnight kiss. She turned towards the basement door and headed down the stairs to her room.

The kitchen seemed unusually quiet after Elta left. The strange comment she had made hung heavily in the air. Letta couldn't help but wonder what her sister had meant by what she said. Why in the world wouldn't she see her tomorrow? Didn't they see each other every day? With a slight shrug of her shoulders she decided to ask Elta the next morning what she meant by her statement.

The next morning dawned with all the freshness of a beautiful spring day. Letta rose early to start washing the clothes. Her tubs were assembled out on the back porch. She leaned over the tubs and set to work. Every now and then as she worked she would pause and sit back to enjoy the gorgeous weather. She glanced periodically over her shoulder expecting to see Elta at any moment. Normally her sister was up by this time to help her hang the clothes.

Letta walked out to the back yard and started hanging up the clothes. Whenever she heard a noise she turned around half expecting to see her sister. It seemed such a shame that Elta was missing out on this beautiful morning. She reached in her basket for a dress and lifted it up to the clothesline when suddenly she remembered the strange comment Elta had made the night before.

"I wonder what she meant by that?" pondered Letta. She stood stock still for a moment feeling a bit of unease over what Elta had said.

She brushed the thought out of her mind and continued her task, but the thought refused to stay away. The more she thought about Elta's strange remark, the more she felt it necessary to run check on Elta.

Letta spun around on her heel and dashed back into the house. She opened the basement door and called down to her sister, "Elta! Elta, is everything alright?"

Silence greeted her question.

She rushed down the stairs to her sister's room and pushed the door open. Elta lay resting peacefully on her bed.

"Elta, honey, are you okay?" Letta asked as she moved across the room to the bed.

Her questions continued to be met with silence.

Her heart told her that her little sister had gone to be with their heavenly Father, but she still reached for her hand, hoping to feel life. She grasped her sister's cold lifeless hand between her warm hands. Instinctively she began to rub the stiff hand with her warm palms.

"Elta, this is what you meant when you said I might not see you," whispered Letta, gently laying her sister's hand down on the bed and lightly brushing her hair away from her face.

Her sister's foreknowledge of her death brought comfort and a sense of peace to Letta's heart. Although she knew she would miss her sister and their daily chats, Letta took her death in stride.

About a year after Elta's death, Margie introduced her parents to Fred Seaward, a young man she had met in Bible School. The young man asked the Hansens if he could have the privilege of marrying their daughter. Everyone saw that God's hand was upon this couple, and so the agreement was given for them to get married.

The Hansens traveled down to California for the wedding. On August 17, 1951, everyone gathered together at Walteria Assembly of God Church for the wedding of Margie and Fred. Letta caught her breath when she saw her little girl dressed in a white satin gown coming down the aisle on the arm of Harold. Harold handed his daughter over to Fred and took his place next to his wife. He reached for her hand and squeezed it reassuringly.

After the wedding they went back up to Okanogan. It wasn't long before Margie and Fred joined them, making their house one of the stops on their honeymoon. They didn't have long to spend there in Washington before

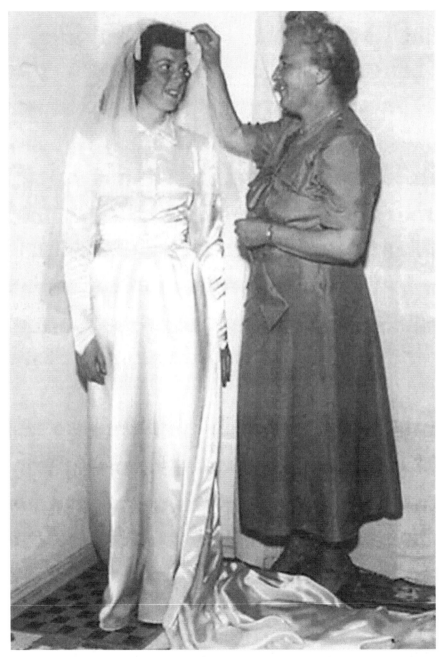

Letta and her daughter Margaret on her wedding day

they had to rush back down to California.

The days tumbled along bringing grandchildren and another wedding. On December 24, 1952, Bud married a wonderful girl named Esther. They gathered in the church in Okanogan for the ceremony.

Gwen soon graduated from nursing school and returned to Washington. She met Fritz Tayet, the principal of Mason Junior High School in Tacoma. What a joyful occasion when Gwen and Fritz Tayet were married. Letta stood back and viewed in amazement what God was doing in her family. He had blessed each of her children with wonderful life partners. Her prayers had been answered above and beyond what she could have ever thought or imagined.

It had always been Letta's prayer to see her children involved in one form of ministry or another. Margie and her husband Fred were very involved as assistant pastors of the church in Walteria. Bud and his wife Esther dived right into an evangelistic ministry. God had given Bud a beautiful singing voice, and he was able to use his talent in the meetings he held. Gwen and Fritz worked together to serve in whatever capacity was necessary in their church. Nothing could have made Letta happier than seeing the way her children were seeking after God and His ways.

In the midst of this portrait of joy was splashed a dab of sadness. Letta's father was battling cancer. She could see that he was suffering from the pain and discomfort. It wasn't easy to see her father in this weakened condition. He had always been such a strong man, and even now despite his physical weakness his inner strength shone through.

Grandpa Teuber seemed to know his time was fast coming to an end, and he wanted to visit his daughter Edith in the nearby county. While he was away visiting them, Margie brought her baby daughter, Debbie, for a month's visit with Letta, who was thrilled to have her youngest daughter around her once again. Letta enjoyed talking with Margie and playing with her new baby granddaughter.

One Saturday morning during their visit, Letta woke up and went straight into the kitchen where Margie was sitting.

"Good morning, Mama," greeted Margie. "Good morning," Letta

responded. "Do you know what I dreamed last night?"

"No, what did you dream?" Margie asked.

"I saw Mama come towards me, and she was dressed in her apron just like in one of her pictures that I had seen her in. As she approached me in the dream, I said, 'Well, Mama, what are you doing here? What brings you here?' and she said, 'Oh, I've come to get Papa. Have you got his things ready?' I asked her, 'Well, when is that going to be?' She said to me, 'Oh, on a Monday.' Now can you imagine what a strange dream that was?"

Letta reached for a cup to make some tea. She moved around the kitchen in silence. Stopping in front of the window, she looked out at the backyard and said thoughtfully, "I think that this dream is saying that Papa, when he does go, it will be on a Monday."

Margie swung Debbie up on her hip and walked over to her mother.

"I think you are right."

The rest of the weekend went by fast. There didn't seem to be enough hours to enjoy all they wanted to do together. Monday came all too quickly and it was time for Margie to fly back to California.

On the way to the airport in Seattle they stopped over in Chelan to see Grandpa Teuber. When they walked into his room he was heavily sedated and seemed to be unconscious. Letta leaned over and kissed him on the cheek.

"Papa, Margie is here to see you," she said.

He was unable to respond to anything that was said to him. They gathered around his bed and prayed together before they left to continue on their way to Seattle.

Harold and Letta stood in the waiting gallery watching the plane get ready to take off. Letta heard something pass between herself and her husband. It sounded like a whoosh of wind.

"Oh, there goes Papa!" She exclaimed.

On their way back home they stopped off at Chelan to check on Grandpa Teuber. Edith ran out the door to met Letta.

She fell into Letta's arms, sobbing, "Papa has gone!"

"Oh, Edith, I know, I know he has gone. He is free from all pain and suffering now that he is in Jesus' arms," Letta comforted her sister.

"Do you know the exact time he died?" she asked Edith.

When they double-checked the time of death, it was the exact time she had sensed something like a spirit moving past her.

The dream she'd had on Saturday came back to her, and she now realized that when her mother had said 'Monday' in the dream it never dawned on her that it would be that very next Monday. Once again she felt a reassurance that God had everything in His hands. She was going to miss her father, but she knew he was in a far better place.

Now Letta and Harold were alone in their large house. After all the years of taking care of so many people, the house felt so very empty. Letta had always been an intercessor, but now she dove deeper into the area of intercession. People knew they could come to her with a need or a problem knowing that she wouldn't just glibly say she would pray for them. She spent hours on her knees beseeching the Lord on behalf of those around her. Time not spent on her knees was spent involved in the lives of the people from their church.

In the spring of 1955, Margie called up to her parents to let them know that she and Fred were praying about going to Singapore. Brother and Sister Rothgam needed a replacement so that they could go on a furlough.

"Please pray with us. We've already laid out a fleece and it has come back positive." Margie said.

"You want to think carefully, Margie. Singapore isn't the kind of place you would want to go unless God is really calling you. The weather there is terrible. The heat is terrible," Harold cautioned her. When they put down the phone, Letta sat quietly thinking about her daughter and this new course she wanted to take. She didn't know quite what to think. The only thing she could remember about Singapore was when the Teia Maru stopped off there to pick up the exchange prisoners of war. It had been a horrid place and those prisoners who got on the ship looked close to death. The whole idea of Singapore brought such horrible memories. She knew she wanted her children to be in the ministry, but somehow she didn't feel very comfortable about them going to Singapore.

The next day during the church prayer time, Letta asked for prayer for

Margie and Fred. Over the next few days she spent much time praying for her children and the important decision they had to make. Anytime there was a group prayer meeting she would bring up her prayer request.

"Please pray for Margaret and Fred, because they are thinking of going to Singapore. Just pray that God will show them what they are really supposed to do."

Brother Rasmussen stood up and said, "Let us pray that Sister Hansen will be willing to let them go."

Letta stared dumbfounded at what had been said. She knew she could not respond with a comment because he had hit the nail on the head. She got down on her knees and asked the Lord to forgive her for not being willing to let them go. She asked Him to help her release her daughter and her family to go wherever He saw fit. In her desire to protect them, she had blinded herself to what God wanted for their lives.

Right before they were to leave for the mission field, Margie and Fred made a trip up to Okanogan. Twenty-three-month-old Debbie and sixteen-month- old Pam toddled into the house, instantly filling it with laughter. Letta found herself wanting to talk them out of their trip, especially since Margie was seven months pregnant with her third child. It just didn't seem to be an appropriate time to be traveling all the way around the world. No matter what she felt, Letta knew she could not change what God had already set in motion.

Their days together sped by in a flash. On the final day of their visit they all said their good-byes. When Margie leaned forward to hug and kiss her father, she clung to him and began to sob uncontrol- lably. It almost seemed unnatural.

Letta said, "Margie, don't carry on like that. Why do you do that?"

"You don't understand; I'll never see him again!" Margie sobbed bitterly.

"Don't be silly, Margie, of course you are going to see your father again," Letta gently chided her daughter.

No one could have understood how Letta's heart ached as she said good-bye, which probably explained why she couldn't bear to hear Margie's heart-wrenching sobs. She was trying so hard not to feel the pain of this parting. Margie had been apart from her for quite some time now, but at least they were still in the same country. Now with her going to such a far away place it seemed almost unbearable.

As was her normal practice, Letta went to the Lord for her comfort. He gave her such peace about everything that she knew there would be nothing to worry about. After the kids reached Singapore, she received wonderful news that Margie had delivered a bouncing baby boy and named him Frederick Oliver Seaward III. She relished each and every letter she got from her daughter telling her of the wonderful things God was doing in Singapore. It thrilled her heart to hear about Debbie, Pam, and Ricky and all the mischief they got into. How she longed to be there with them.

Harold's health deteriorated over the next few months. After much prayer they decided they needed to give up the pastorate of the Okanogan church. They decided to move down to the sunnier climate of Southern California. Fred and Margie's small two-bedroom house in Lomita was available, so they made arrangements to move in.

Gone were the beautiful green hills that Letta loved. Now when she stepped outside her front door she just looked straight into another house across the street. She wasn't used to the rows and rows of houses lining the streets of Lomita; yet even in this place, she knew God was with her.

Harold's health continued to decline, yet he still kept involved in the Harbor City Foursquare Church where he became the assistant pastor. He and Letta attended the services regularly and offered what- ever help they could give. Letta loved the fact that they always worked as a team. God had done such a wonderful job of choosing the right life partner for her.

The Harbor Christian School asked Letta to come on staff as the registrar of the school. Letta was never one to step away from a challenge, so she agreed to take the job. She found herself immersed in the lives of so many people, and she was happy that this gave her ample opportunities to share the love of her Lord Jesus.

She persuaded Harold Jr. (Bud) to come down and help teach at the school. He moved down to Lomita with his wife Esther and their two sons Jon and Jim. The two little boys were a delight to be around, and Letta enjoyed getting to be an overindulgent grandmother to them.

Towards the end of 1958, Harold's health weakened rapidly. His heart problems and other physical ailments left him almost bedridden. It got to the point where Harold's heavy 6'2" frame became too difficult for Letta to handle on her own. One day as she was trying to help him get up from the bed, she found she had no strength to lift him up. Letta knew there was no other choice except to let him go to a hospital.

The day Harold was put in the hospital, Letta stayed with him until dusk fell, and then she went home. As she opened the door to their little house and walked in, she was immediately overcome by the emptiness in the house. It had been many years since she was alone, and she found that it was not easy to be reunited with this old stranger, loneliness. She hurried to her bedroom and fell to her knees by the bed. She sought solace in the friend that would never leave her nor forsake her. He would never leave her alone, and He would always be there with her no matter what was ahead.

She started a daily routine, waking up and going to the hospital to sit next to Harold where she could read her Bible to him and talk to him. After spending time with him, she would rush over to the school to perform her duties. Immediately after school, she rushed back to spend more time with her husband. She would tell him about her day, and then they would pray together. They prayed over any needs or problems that had arisen during the day.

Whenever a letter came from one of the children she would read it to him. One day Letta came into his room happily waving a letter.

"Oh look, Harold, a letter from the kids in Singapore!" Letta exclaimed.

He turned his head and smiled at her, "Read it, dear. Tell me how they are."

She opened the envelope and took out the letter. A quick glance over the contents of the letter brought a shout of "Glory" from her lips.

Attempting to lean forward, Harold asked weakly, ""What is it?"

"They are coming home. They will be here in December!"

He fell back on his pillow with a big smile plastered on his face. Letta looked over at her husband and smiled.

Harold Jr. visited his father regularly in the hospital. His father only wanted him to read more of the Word of God to him. Letta would sit quietly by as her son read chapter after chapter from the Bible. She could see that her husband was more interested in hearing the Word of God than being involved in needless chatter. He couldn't get enough of the reading of the Bible. He wanted to spend his time meditating on what had been read and discussing it with Harold Jr. and Letta.

On December 28, 1958, Letta woke up early. She glanced at the alarm clock and realized she needed to hurry if she wanted to see Harold before she had to get ready for church. She loved being there when he woke up in the morning, helping him eat his breakfast. Throwing on a simple dress, she dashed out the door.

Gently pushing open the hospital room door, Letta peeked in to see whether Harold was awake. His head turned to the sound of the door opening and he smiled feebly. Letta moved across the room to his bed.

"Good morning," greeted Letta.

Leaning forward to adjust his pillows, she continued, "Do you realize it will only be ten more days until the children come home?"

He nodded weakly, taking a sip of the water she offered him. After he had finished eating his breakfast, she glanced at her watch.

"Look at the time! I need to go and get ready for church."

"Oh, do you have to go? Why can't you stay here with me?" Harold pleaded.

She looked at her husband and replied, "You know I need to go to church, and I will come over right after the service is done."

She bent down and kissed him and then turned to leave. Just as Letta reached the door, Harold called out, "Remember, the dead in Christ shall rise first!"

Letta dashed home and got herself ready for church. Walking towards the door to leave, the phone rang. She debated on whether or not to answer it; she glanced at her watch and realized she was late. Nonetheless she turned and reached for the phone. The hospital was on the other end of the line. Her heart sank when she heard them tell her that Harold had passed away. The phone slid out of her hands and back into the cradle. She moved mechanically across the room towards the open front door. Her mind wrestled with the fact that he was really gone.

The scenery slipped by her unnoticed on her way back to the hospital. Harold's last words repeated over and over in her mind, "Remember, the dead in Christ shall rise first!" Harold always said he would be going to be with Jesus by way of the rapture and not by way of the grave. When he had made that statement to her in the hospital earlier, he was trying to tell her that now he knew he was going by way of the grave and it was okay with him. He accepted whatever God had for him; she needed to accept what God had for her.

The next few days moved by in a whirlwind of activity. Arrangements for the funeral had to be made and people needed to be informed. Marge and her family were still out at sea and a message needed to be sent to them to let them know about Harold's death. Now it all made sense, the tearful parting that Marge had with Harold. Her spirit must have sensed that she would not see her father alive again.

Letta asked Harold Jr. to send the message to Marge out on the boat. Just the thought of her daughter receiving the message brought back painful memories of the message she had received long ago of her mother's passing.

Letta walked through every day in a sort of daze. She had been taking care of so many people over the last ten years and now there was no one left to take care of. First Elta had gone, and then Papa, and now her beloved Harold. The world kept spinning, but for Letta everything in her life stopped. In the midst of all the uproar of funeral arrangements and friends coming by, a heavy blanket of loneliness descended upon Letta.

Marge and family arrived and crowded into the tiny house with their four children. The children had come at a good time. If only they could crowd out the deep sense of loneliness that Letta felt.

The New Year came, and Letta folded her blanket of loneliness and tucked it away carefully in the recesses of her heart. She busied herself with her children and grandchildren. Marge asked her if she wanted to go up to visit Gwen in Washington. It was such a wonderful idea. She would get a chance to see Gwen and her son Rodney, who was almost two, and Gwen's newborn baby. The visit was wonderful, and Harold Jr. and family met them there, so it turned out to be an impromptu reunion. Letta stood back and observed her children with a heart filled with thanksgiving. Their lives had far exceeded her expectations. They were such good children and they had grown into marvelous parents.

On her return to California, Letta settled back into a comfortable routine. She was still working at the school. After her work hours, she remained active in church and helping out with the family. The months slipped by, and before she knew it her sixty-first birthday had come and gone.

A couple weeks later, on Sunday, April 29, 1959, Letta clambered out of bed. After getting herself ready for church, she made her way to the kitchen to eat breakfast. Marge was already up preparing breakfast for everyone. Letta opened the cupboard and reached for a coffee cup. Holding the cup in her hands, she turned around to face Marge and said thoughtfully, "I had a very strange dream last night. I really believe it's from the Lord, but I don't understand the meaning of the dream. I wonder if you can help me."

Marge agreed to try to help her mother figure out the dream. Letta went on to explain her dream:

"I dreamt that I was sitting in church during one of the services when suddenly Daddy (Harold) was there, and yet I knew he wasn't there in person. It was like he was a faint shadow of his being and was standing right behind me. He wasn't sitting beside me; he was standing behind me just looking at me and shaking his head saying, 'Poor Letta, poor Letta.' Right then two hands came down from heaven and put this package in my lap, and even though I was in church it seemed to me it was proper that I should open the package; actually, there were really two packages, a large one and a smaller one fastened together. When I opened the larger package it had a dress, and when I opened the little one it had the under slip to go with the dress. Inside the small one there was a tiny silver-wrapped package, and on that silver-wrapped package there was a little note. The note said, "From one who cares." When I opened up the silver package it had a little handkerchief inside. Daddy was still there shaking his head and saying, 'Poor Letta.' And that was the end of the dream. I have no idea what it means!"

Letta turned to Marge to see if she had any idea what the dream could mean. Marge just stared at her and shook her head.

"Sorry, Mama, I can't make any sense of the dream either," Margie replied. They hurried with the breakfast cleanup and rushed off to church. After the service was over, Letta felt very tired and crawled into bed for a short afternoon nap. She fell into a sound sleep. When she woke up from her nap she felt renewed.

She walked out into the living room and saw Fred and Marge sitting close together on the couch. They seemed unusually quiet. They both looked up at her when she entered the room, and she knew by the looks on their faces that something was wrong.

"Mama, please sit down," Marge advised her mother.

She stood up and walked towards her mother. "What is it, Margie?" Letta asked.

There was a pregnant pause, and then Margie cleared her throat, "Mama, while you were asleep there was a phone call...."

"Go on, tell me what it is all about," Letta urged her daughter.

Marge was definitely uncomfortable and glanced over to Fred for support. She took a deep breath and started up where she left off.

"Do you remember Gwen's brother-in-law having a yacht? Well, they decided to take it on a trial run today. They had gone to Sunday school, but after Sunday school they left to take the yacht out on the Puget Sound..."

Letta interrupted Marge, "But on a Sunday? Gwen knows better than that! Sunday is the Lord's day."

"I know Mama, just listen... I'm not done yet.

While they were out on the yacht with quite a big group, I think about twelve people, the boat sprang a leak and it sank, Mama. The boat sank. Most of the passengers were drowned. Little Rodney was picked up by a helicopter and he is recovering, but Mama, Gwen is gone!" Marge stopped waiting for her words to sink in.

"No!" cried Letta, "Gwen is a good swimmer. She can't be gone!"

"She's gone! Oh Mama, I'm so sorry. Mama, don't you see it is the dream you had."

Letta looked puzzled.

"What do you mean; what does it have to do with my dream?" She asked.

Marge went on to explain, "Don't you see, the package came to you while you were in church. Mama, the accident happened while you were in church this morning. The dress and the slip are two separate garments but they really belong together; a husband and wife are two separate people but they belong together. That is Gwen and Fritz, Mama. The little tiny package with the handkerchief was their baby, little Jana Lynn. The handkerchief shows you that God shall wipe away all tears. Oh Mama, I'm so sorry!"

Tears were washing down Letta's face as she listened to her daughter explain the dream. It all made perfect sense to her now. That dream had definitely been given to her from the Lord.

"Margie, it said on the gift, 'from one who cares.' He cares for me. He wants me to know that He loves me." Her tears began to wash away the years of pain she had kept carefully hidden away deep inside.

She quietly repeated the phrase over and over again. Each time the words were said, they eroded away the bitterness and questioning that had been so carefully concealed in her spirit. Letta looked over at Marge and began to explain to her what was happening in her inner spirit.

"For years now I have buried my pain from the loss of baby Viola. I could never understand why God took her away from me. Now with this dream I have had, and with Gwen dying suddenly like this, somehow I am completely free from all that questioning. I can see things in a different light altogether. There is no need to question anymore, because He cares for me. Whatever comes in my life, it comes from the one who cares." Letta's spirit grew increasingly lighter as she continued to explain herself to her daughter.

Over the next few days she kept repeating the phrase "from one who cares" to herself. It gave her courage to go on, and she needed all the strength and courage she could get. They set off for Washington to attend the funeral. Their last visit had been a wonderful family reunion, and now Letta was coming to bury her eldest daughter.

Walking into the slumber room of the funeral home, Letta wasn't prepared for the sight that met her eyes. Five caskets stood side by side, lining the room. There had been seven people who lost their lives on that fateful Sunday. One of the bodies was lost in the waters, and amongst the remaining six was Gwen's eight-month-old baby.

Letta walked past each casket looking for Gwen. She kept remembering the dream and it helped her to keep herself together. She came to a casket with a mother and a little baby snuggled in her arms. The woman in the casket didn't look anything like Gwen; her face was disfigured from the trauma of drowning. Letta stood looking in at her daughter and once again the dream came to her mind. In the dream the little package was in the package with the slip; how appropriate that Gwen's baby should be nestled in her arms in the casket.

Others were milling around the room weeping uncontrollably. Letta moved amongst them comforting them and helping them during their time of need. It amazed others to see her so strong. They knew she had just lost her husband and now she'd lost her eldest daughter, but she was the one giving reassurance and comfort to those around her. She comforted herself by saying, "It's from one who cares, and He knows best."

After the funeral was over and she had come back home to California, Letta sensed that she was about to embark on a whole new chapter of her life. The way ahead was not clear, but she had no fears. She knew that her Master and Savior Jesus had already navigated the waters before her, and He would guide her safely through.

13

The time came for Fred and Marge to head back to Singapore. They asked Letta to accompany them back to Singapore. Whenever she tried to consider going she would just see a black curtain in front of her, so she declined their offer. Once again she had to say good-bye to her daughter, wishing her all of God's blessings.

She was uncertain as to what God wanted her to do; in the meantime, she kept involved with whatever task He brought across her path. Her time of service had not come to an end. To others she looked like she had done more than enough for God in her life, but God had other plans for her.

In May 1961, Harold Jr. was invited to take over the pastorate of a church in Hawaii. He asked his mother to join him in the work in Hawaii, and she felt a definite release in her spirit to go with her son. Harold and Esther and their three children, Jon, Jim and Cheryl went to Hawaii together with Letta. She helped out in the church and around the home.

During her stay in Hawaii she developed a serious kidney problem. Her condition deteriorated and no one expected her to pull through. There was a nurse to take care of her twenty-four hours a day. After ten days of gradually getting worse, Letta felt low in her spirit and thought that it must be her time to die. It was a Sunday morning and everyone had left for church.

While she was lying there in her bed, Letta heard footsteps coming down the hallway of the parsonage towards her door. She positioned her head so that she could see who would be coming in through the door.

I wonder who is coming. They should be in church; why would they come and see me? she kept thinking.

She closed her eyes and opened them again, and to her surprise she saw Jesus standing in front of her.

Struggling to lift her head up, she said, "Oh, have You come to take me?"

He replied, "No, I have just come to visit with you."

He went on to tell her that when it was her time to go, He would let her know. At this moment, He had come just to talk to her.

He lifted up his hands and she saw that he was holding a seed bag. He asked her if she wanted to sow the seeds.

"How can I? I'm so weak; I can't even lift my head off this pillow. How can I?" she responded.

He just offered her the seed bag and said again,

"Won't you sow the seed?"

Again she responded, "But I can't, I'm so weak."

Suddenly the room in front of her disappeared and she was given a vision. In the vision she saw herself in an area that had palm trees. She was standing there on a hillside. She saw a Chinese man come into the scene and another fellow hold him by the throat and strangle him until his eyes were bulging out. His face began to turn purple in color.

She just stood looking at what was going on.

Jesus said to her, "Aren't you going to do anything?"

She said, "I can't. I'm too weak."

"Aren't you going to even say something?" He asked her.

She immediately spoke to the man in the vision who was choking the Chinese man. "Don't do that! You can't do that!"

He dropped his victim and turned to her with his hands stretched out towards her. He moved forward as if he was going to strangle her.

"Don't you know I could choke you to death?" He snarled.

She said, "Yes, I know you could do that to me, but you can't do it to the One standing beside me."

He took one look at the Lord Jesus and he dropped on all fours and scuttled out of the scene.

The Chinese man stood up full of joy because he had been set free from the oppressor.

The scene vanished. Once again Jesus offered her the seed bag, and this time she agreed to take it. As she reached for the bag, she felt healing flowing through her body. It was almost an instantaneous healing. She was able to get up from her bed, and when Harold Jr. and the family returned from church she told them what God had done.

She knew that God was telling her she needed to go back into the harvest field. When she had thought of going to Singapore in the past, something would always hold her back. Now there was a release from that restraint, and she knew that she needed to prepare herself to go and be with Marge and Fred Seaward in Singapore. She talked with her son about her decision, and he gave her his blessing.

In October of 1962, Letta made her way to Singapore. A blast of hot air met Letta as she emerged from the small aircraft. As she walked across the tarmac, she glanced around at the palm trees and the lush greenery; the island was beautiful.

Marge was at the waiting area to greet her. Hugs and kisses abounded as they made up for the time they had been separated from each other.

"You children have grown!" Letta said, as she hugged each of her five grandchildren.

The whole family piled into their Volkswagen van. Letta sat in the back seat with Marge catching up on all that had been going on. As they drove along, she would glance out the window and catch sight of the people milling through the streets. The majority of the Singapore population was Chinese, so she felt as though she had come 'home.' Tears sprang to her eyes as she remembered Jesus offering her the seed bag. She knew she was here to continue sowing the seed.

The van pulled into the driveway of the church. The church building was a two-story building that had been a former school. The children clambered out of the van and ran on ahead to the back of the building. Letta and Marge walked slowly behind them along a small pathway that led to the rear of the building. As they rounded the building, they walked past some doors and came to a large wooden door. Fred pushed opened the door and put Letta's luggage in the center of the room.

"This is your room, Mama." Marge said.

The room was spacious with a door connecting it to a garage. The garage was where barrels and other luggage were stored. Letta smiled contentedly as she looked around her room.

In the car she had told Marge about the visit she had from Jesus and the fact that Jesus would let her know when it was her time to go. Now that they were alone in the room, Marge said to her, "Be sure you let me know if the Lord ever tells you. Don't you just keep it a secret; I want to know what is going on!"

Letta looked up to see the children lingering around the doorway. "Come on in kids. Don't just stand there, come on in and help Grandma unpack." It didn't take a second invitation before the children all ran in to be with their Grandma. They were so excited to have her with them in Singapore, and she was equally excited to see them again.

"Now you will have to refresh my memory. I need to know how old each of you is." Letta smiled.

Debbie stepped forward and said, "I'm ten years old."

Then she turned and pointed to Pam, "She is eight, Rick is seven and Doug is four."

"That leaves your youngest sister, and how old is she?" asked Letta.

"She is one and a half." Pam announced with a big grin.

The moment Letta landed in Singapore she became "Grandma Hansen" not only to her grandchildren, but also to everyone else in the church. She began a great ministry of teaching, preaching and counseling. People would come to her every day needing to pour out their problems to her. They knew that she would listen carefully and give them good counsel. She prayed earnestly with them, and after they left, she would continue to intercede on their behalf for their various needs.

Fred and Marge had two churches they were taking care of. The main

The Seaward family at Bethel Assembly of God, 1966

church was Bethel Assembly of God and the outreach church they had started was called Calvary Assembly of God. There was so much ministry opportunity in both churches. Fred invited her to preach at both churches. The people in the church loved to hear her preach. She always had an anointed message when she stood up to share God's Word.

Aside from preaching and counseling, she got involved teaching individuals in the church. She had a series of personal Bible Study materials that she used in teaching. The whole series took about six months to teach each student. Each of her students would come for their lesson once a week. They would come and spend about 45 minutes to one hour with her and she would expound on the Word of God. These lessons caused them to be grounded in their faith. She knew she was fulfilling Christ's command to go and make disciples of all the nations ... teaching them to observe all that He commanded. Letta understood the importance of not only getting people saved, but also teaching them all that He had commanded. She never grew weary with the teaching.

One morning when Letta woke up she felt unusually sick. She decided she needed to rest a bit before one of her students came by for his lesson. By the time the student arrived at the house, her condition had worsened.

Fred met the student outside her door and said, "I'm sorry George, but Grandma Hansen is too ill to be able to teach you today."

A weak voice drifted out through the doorway. "Never mind, Fred, send him in, send him in."

Letta moved herself up in the bed and taught him right from her bed. She didn't want to allow anything to hinder her from fulfilling the mission God had given her. He had renewed the call on her heart and she was just overwhelmed by His faithfulness. After all these years, He still could use her.

In the midst of all her teaching, preaching and counseling, she never neglected her intercessory prayer. She prayed for each of her students and those in the church. Whenever she heard of a need or a problem, she made sure that she would lift it up to God in prayer. She didn't stop praying for something until she felt a complete breakthrough.

Letta's body was getting older, but her spirit got stronger. Even when she was faced with heart prob- lems, she just kept right on going. At one point she was laid up in bed for almost six weeks. The church people would visit her and pray over her. Marge and Fred would come in and pray over her, but it just seemed as though they couldn't get the victory over the sickness.

Letta felt a bit discouraged and longed for her son Harold Jr., as God used him in the area of physical healing. As she lay in bed one day, she picked up her Bible and flipped the pages over to the Psalms. She scanned the page and suddenly a verse just jumped out at her:

"He sent His Word and healed them."

That Word became alive and spoke to her spirit. She jumped up from the bed shouting, "I'm healed! I'm healed!"

After six weeks of not being able to get up from her sick bed, suddenly God reached down and sent His Word to her. It was as if the Lord was saying, "You don't need this one or that one and the other one praying for you; you just need My Word."

Letta moved around her room touching every part of her body. She was totally healed.

She rejoiced at the goodness of God. He was indeed her healer.

Letta carried a very special anointing. Maybe it was because she had been so broken in her life. Whatever it was, those around her could always feel a special realm of the spirit when they were around her. She had a soft nature, so loving and kind. When she spoke to people she spoke with sweet kindness, yet with such an authority. Those in the church loved to be around her to listen to what she had to say.

There were many teenagers in the church. Despite the vast age difference, they were drawn to Grandma Hansen. There was a young man whose life had been totally transformed when he came to know Jesus. His old lifestyle consisted of fighting and gangs. Now all he wanted was to be close to God. He had a lovely girlfriend and they were very happy in their relationship with one another. One day they had a big quarrel that caused a rift in their relation- ship. It seemed like there would be no way for them to come back together. Letta took time to sit down with them and counsel them. She worked with them and helped them get back together. It amazed them that this older woman cared enough to take time to work through their problems with them. The couple soon was married and went on to work together as a dynamic team to do mighty exploits for God.

There was no doubt in anybody's mind that Letta loved people. God used her love for people to touch so many lives. Young and old alike never were the same after meeting up with Grandma Hansen. If they were in a meeting and she gave a word of prophecy, they would feel the presence of God move through the whole place. At times the young people in the church would grow cold in their hearts. Some of them backslid and were just going to church out of formality or routine. God used Letta to speak forth words of prophecy that would cause those in the service to weep and cry out to God for forgiveness.

God gave Letta dreams and visions. She trusted Him to lead her in every area of her life. Through the dreams and visions, she was often burdened to intercede for others.

One night she had a dream of graves, a multitude of tombstones. Suddenly they opened up and out came different people from the church. Some of those who came out of the graves were some young people from the church who had backslidden. She woke up and told Fred and Marge the dream.

"I believe the Lord is showing us that those who have gone away from Him are going to come back to Him. They are going to be revived spiritually. Don't stop praying for them. They are going to be revived!" Letta proclaimed.

Letta never gave up praying for those she had seen in the dream. Sure enough, one by one each of those individuals did come back to the Lord.

Letta's life was not filled with religiosity. Her faith was genuine and it permeated every area of her life. God was involved in every facet of her life. She didn't put on a Sunday outfit and suddenly become anointed just for the services. Her anointing carried over even into the home. Everything she did, she did for God. Marge found her mother an inspiration to be around. She always had just the right thing to say.

She knew when to talk and when to keep quiet.

In the mornings, after her devotion time, she would join Marge in the kitchen area of the house. As Marge moved around preparing the breakfast, Letta flowed right along helping wherever she was needed. Marge looked forward to every moment she spent with her mother. Going off to Bible College when she was sixteen had cut her time with her mother short; now she wanted to glean everything she could from her mother's wisdom and grace.

One morning Letta watched as Marge rushed around getting things ready. She was in her normal "go, go, go" mode. She never gave herself a chance and was always very hard on herself.

Letta turned to Marge and said, "Marge, the Holy Spirit doesn't drive us, He leads us. You need to really pray and ask the Lord whether this is of the Lord or if this is of the devil and your flesh, because the Holy Spirit will not drive you. He leads you gently and He doesn't drive you."

It sounded so simple and yet it was so profound. Marge knew immediately that what her mother had to say was right. She loved the way her mother knew exactly what was wrong in a situation. More than anything she appreciated the fact that Letta didn't needlessly jump into the private affairs between Marge and Fred. Whenever a disagreement arose between the two of them, Letta would quietly walk out of the room and leave them to settle the matter. If the children misbehaved or if they had a need, she would go to Marge privately and tell her what she felt about the child.

Despite various battles with sickness and disease, Letta continued to labor steadfastly for the Lord. Each new battle of sickness just proved to be another victory for her to testify of God's goodness and His healing power.

Anytime she would get sick, Marge would ask her, "Now, Mama, has the Lord showed you that it's your time?"

If she replied no, then Marge would feel full of faith and go ahead and pray. She was so sure that God would reveal to her mother when it was her time to go.

One day when Marge and Letta were alone together, Letta felt pressure across her chest. She took a deep breath but she couldn't get enough air. She struggled to breathe as the vice around her chest tightened.

Marge's eyes widened with fear as she realized her mother was fighting for air. She jumped up and grabbed a magazine to fan her with it.

"Oh, Jesus, help me. What do I do? I don't know what to do for her!" She cried.

Everything swirled around in front of Letta, and she slumped back in her chair. She could still hear her daughter, but she couldn't respond. Marge continued fanning her mother as she fell to her knees and cried out again, "Oh, Jesus, help me! I don't even know how to pray, Jesus."

She said, "Mama, has the Lord shown you this is your time to go?"

Letta shook her head weakly, indicating that He hadn't told her it was time to go. She felt Marge change in her stance. A power descended upon her as she jumped to her feet praying in tongues. Letta felt Marge's hands on her head, and she heard her rebuking the enemy. She boldly battled against the foe. As she continued to pray, Letta took a deep breath and felt the air filling her lungs. Another breath followed and she felt her strength slowly come back.

A great excitement filled the room as both mother and daughter joined together to thank God for His healing touch. It had always been a great fear for Marge that she would be alone with her mother when she became really ill. She had stood up to the horrible fear and witnessed how God intervened and brought victory.

God continued to see Letta through even the darkest of moments. She knew that no matter what valley she walked through, He never would let go of her hand. Despite her various ailments and afflictions, she was determined to keep walking close to her Savior, Jesus.

One day she went out with Fred and Marge in the Volkswagen van. She and Marge were enjoying themselves talking together in the backseat. They were so engrossed in their conversation they never even looked out the window. Suddenly a man on a bicycle appeared out of nowhere and darted out in front of the van. Fred didn't even have time to warn the women. He slammed on the brakes and they flew forward off the seat.

Marge looked around in a daze. She slid herself back up on the seat and dusted herself off. She still wasn't sure what had happened. Unfortunately, Letta couldn't move. She had been flung against the front seats of the van and she was in extreme pain.

They sped to the hospital. The doctors examined Letta's hip and confirmed that it had been broken. The doctor told Letta that she would need to have a pin in her hip, but she refused to have it done.

No one could understand why she was so stubborn about getting a pin put in her hip. When she was pressed further on the issue, Letta explained that her mother had a pin put in her hip and that was the end of her. Letta was firm in her decision to simply trust God for her healing.

As a result of her decision, Letta was confined to her bed. Marge took care of her and brought her meals to her bedroom. She continued her teaching and counseling from her bed. The only thing she couldn't do was go to church.

John Hague, a young man in the British armed forces, came in to talk to her one day. He had been saved in the church and was on fire for God. Grandma Hansen had been instrumental in his life, and he longed to do something in return.

John began by saying, "Grandma Hansen, let me tell you something strange."

He took a deep breath and continued on, "You haven't been able to come to church and enjoy the services with us, so I was planning to rig up a sound system. I even had figured out exactly how much wiring I would need to run the system all the way back here to your room from the front of the church. With this sound system you would be able to hear the messages and everything that went on during the services. I tell you, I had it all figured out, but when I planned to start setting it up, God distinctly told me not to do it. He told me that if I did it you would depend on it and you would never get well."

He stopped and shook his head.

"I'm sorry I can't do this for you. God must know that you would depend on it and then you wouldn't get well."

Letta told him it was okay. It did seem strange that God wouldn't let her enjoy the services in her room, but she recognized that her Father knew exactly what He was doing. She just rested in His plan.

Everyday she kept herself busy with prayer, reading the Bible, and teaching. There was a neverending stream of visitors coming for prayer or just to talk to her.

Special services were being organized in the church. Letta felt something inside her spirit telling her she needed to go for those meetings.

She called Fred into the room and said, "Please take me into the service."

He gathered together some young men from the church. They fastened their arms together to make a chair for Grandma to sit in. With much maneuvering and a great deal of pain, Letta was able to position herself in the makeshift chair. As they walked towards the church hall, every bounce brought a grimace to her face.

"Oh, Mama, maybe you shouldn't do this!" Marge said.

"I must go." She replied. "I just feel I must go to the service. I can't stay in my room today; I have to get into that service."

They carried her into the main hall and put her down gently right on the front row. Letta bit her lip as she tried to adjust herself to relieve a bit of the pain. Every move she made sent pain shooting through her body.

The service started and the singing brought tears to Letta's eyes. Oh how she had missed being in the house of the Lord. How she had longed to be here with her fellow brothers and sisters enjoying the presence of God in unity.

During a short lull in the worship somebody spoke out a prophetic word from the Lord based on the book of Revelation. The word talked about the river of life that flows from the throne of God. It went on to say that God makes all things new. It was such a beautiful message. As soon as it ended, Letta let out a shout.

"I'm healed! I'm healed!"

She had been instantly healed and she jumped up and walked around. Needless to say the power of God fell on the whole church and they began to rejoice in what God had done. Letta was able to walk from then on without any problems at all. God touched her body and completely healed her.

Each time she was healed her faith would increase to pray for others for their healing. She prayed with real compassion because she had been through the suffering herself. She understood what it was like to live day in and day out with pain. Her prayer life grew richer with every trial she went through.

One of the trials she had to endure was a sickness affecting her stomach. She started noticing that certain foods would not sit well on her stomach. Before too long this happened no matter what she ate. She was unable to keep food down. The little food she kept in her stomach gave her great discom- fort. At first she tried to keep eating with the rest of the family, but it just wasn't working out. Just the thought of food made her stomach turn inside out.

Marge had to prepare special foods for her. She would grind up food into a paste similar to baby's food. It wasn't only the consistency that mattered. If the wrong types of food were mixed up for her they would just wreak havoc on her stomach. Milk and milk products seemed to settle well on her stomach. Letta couldn't help wondering what was wrong with her. She cried out to God for healing, but none came. She dug into the Word of God and clung to every promise she could find. She knew how busy Marge was and she felt bad that she was burdening her with all this special food preparation.

On a Sunday afternoon Marge came into her room and said, "Mama, I just don't know what to do."

"What is it, hon?" Letta asked.

"You know we are going to Frazer's Hill and I just don't know what we are going to do about your food!" Marge was beside herself. "The food is rich and I'm not allowed to use the kitchen up there. I just don't know how we are going to work this out."

Letta smiled, "Don't worry about me."

God knew she needed to go with the children on this vacation; He must know what to do about the food problem. She just had to leave everything up to Him. Had He failed her in the past? No, He had never failed her! He was always faithful. He had proven Himself to her time and time again. Without giving the matter another thought, she dressed herself for the evening service.

In the middle of the Sunday evening meeting, Fred felt impressed to give an altar call for those who were sick. He announced to the church members, "I just feel in my spirit that those of you who are not well should come forward and we'll pray for you. We will ask the Lord to reach down and heal you."

Letta jumped up and stood in the altar area in front of the pulpit. Fred moved around the pulpit and motioned to several of the church members to join them up at the front. They all gathered around and laid hands on Letta.

One of the people praying for her stopped and began to share a vision he had received.

In the vision the Lord showed him the inside of her stomach. He could see round balls the size of golf balls fixed to the inside lining of her stomach. Suddenly, in the vision, those growths just disappeared.

After the vision was shared, everyone said, "In Jesus' name you are healed!"

Letta walked back to her seat. Although she didn't feel any differently in her body, she claimed her healing based on the vision that had been received.

That night she crawled into bed and once again she claimed her healing. The next morning she woke up feeling like something had happened.

She went to the kitchen and told the rest of the family, "I just feel for a good breakfast."

They hadn't heard her say that in such a long time, they all just started laughing. How marvelous to see the healing that God had performed. In His time, He had made all things beautiful.

She had experienced healing in every form possible. She had even received healing after she was prayed over by a young child. One time when she was very ill her youngest granddaughter, Connie, who was four at the time, burst into her room. She ran up to Letta and said, "Grandma, I came to pray for you."

Laying her little hand on Letta's head she said, "Jesus, heal Grandma."

"Good-bye Grandma!" she said as she scampered out the door.

Healing flowed through Letta's body and she was able to get up from her sickbed healed.

Despite her struggles in Singapore, her time there was fruitful. She touched so many lives. God worked in and through her to accomplish His work. She clutched the seed bag firmly as she marched forward sowing the seeds He had given her.

14

Letta enjoyed her time in Singapore. Her burden for the Chinese people had been with her since she was a child. Now as a grandmother, she had the privilege to come to a country where there was an abundance of Chinese people. She conversed in fluent Mandarin and found that many doors were opened to her due to her proficiency in the language.

Before she knew it, two and a half years had flown by. It was time to go back to the United States for a furlough. Although she looked forward to seeing her son Harold and his family, she knew she was going to miss Singapore and the people she had come to love there.

Fred made arrangements for the whole family to sail back on a freighter. They worked night and day in the garage preparing for their departure. Letta's room was connected to the garage by a small door. She moved in and out of the garage helping to pack up things for the trip.

One day as she was going into the garage, she felt God saying something to her. She walked over to a barrel and leaned against it. She said, "What is it Lord?"

"Prepare yourself; you will be coming home before Christmas."

"Mama!" Marge's voice drifted in from the other room.

Letta walked back into the room. Her face had an unusual glow. The minute Marge saw her face, she said, "Mama, has the Lord told you something?"

She nodded and said, "Yes, He has." "What did He tell you?" she asked.

"He said it would be before Christmas," Letta answered.

Marge thought to herself, "Christmas, I have at least until Christmas to be with Mama."

"It will be before Christmas," Letta repeated herself.

Sunday morning as Letta sat in the church service, God showed her a vision of an army of people. The people were marching in a parade. Each person held on to a post, one on one side of the street and one person on the other side. Between the two posts was a big banner. Those in the parade marched down the street. Letta saw herself holding up one of the poles. A voice spoke to her and she recognized it as God's voice. He said, "It is now time; you can put your post down."

Letta protested, "Oh Lord, I can't put it down until I know who will take it up. I can't desert my post. Who will take up my post if I put down the post?"

The Lord said, "Pam will take up the post."

After the service she went to Marge and shared with her the vision God had given her.

"Oh, Mama, I think you've got it wrong. Pam isn't keen about the things of God." Marge told Letta.

"No, the Lord told me that it would be Pam. You mark my words, Margie." Letta said firmly as she turned to go to her room.

The day for their departure arrived all too quickly. They stood on the dock with all the beloved church members who had come to wish them a safe journey. Fred gathered everyone in a big circle. Someone prayed. At the end of the prayer, everyone sang the song, "God Be with You 'Til We Meet Again." The song brought to her remembrance many other boat trips she had made. Every one of those trips carried her to another stage of her life. Now she was going to be embarking on a final voyage. When she said good-bye to these precious people, she would not see them again until they reached heaven's shore.

The song ended and it was time to move up the gangplank.

Letta didn't feel very well the first few days on the ship. She remained in her cabin most of the time trying to adjust to the movement of the ocean. How it brought back memories of her very first voyage across the Pacific Ocean. She had left her home and her family to travel to a land she had never seen. Now forty-five years later she was crossing the Pacific Ocean to return home for the last time.

As soon as she was well, Letta made every effort to spend time with Marge and her family. The weeks spent on the ship sped by and before long it was August and they had docked in San Pedro, California. There on the docks was Harold Jr. waiting eagerly to be reunited with his mother. Harold took Letta up to Omak, Washington to spend time with his family. When she arrived at Harold's house the children rushed out to greet her. How wonderful it was to see them! Jon was eleven, Jim had just turned ten, and little Cheryl was four years old.

Letta used the next couple of months to make sure that everything was in order in her life. She would start each day offering her day to God and asking Him what He wanted her to do. She didn't want to take a step without Him, just as it says in Psalm 119:114:

"You are my hiding place and my shield; I wait for Thy Word."

She knew that as long as she waited for His Word, she would be safe and protected.

One morning as she was praying, she had a vision. In the vision she saw a door. When she walked through the door there was a tunnel leading down to a long flight of stairs. As she descended the staircase, each stair got darker. She kept moving slowly down- wards until she was in complete darkness. As she stepped off the bottom step a brilliant light flooded the scene. The bright light surrounded her. Suddenly she found herself standing on a mountaintop.

When the vision passed, Letta got up from her knees and went out to look for Harold Jr. to tell him about it. She narrated the vision to him and asked him what he thought of it. He looked down at the table and started tracing an invisible line. Finally he looked up at his mother and said, "I believe the

Lord is going to take you home soon, and that you won't be here very long."

Letta smiled and said, "I know you are right. That is exactly what I thought it meant, but I wanted to get a confirmation."

That night Letta said goodnight to everyone and went into her room. She sat on her bed and marveled at the wonderful ways of God. He meant what He said in Jeremiah 33:3: "Call to Me and I will answer you, and I will tell you great and mighty things, which you do not know." She had called on Him so many times in her life, and He had never failed her. He was always there to show her what to do and where to go. Often His timing wasn't her timing, but she had come to see that His timing was always the best. His faithfulness to her had been great, and now she prayed that it would reach to her children and her grandchildren and to their children.

The next morning Letta suffered a heart attack and had to be rushed to the hospital. She faded in and out of consciousness over the next few days. Harold called down to Marge and told her about their mother's condition. She made immediate arrangements to go and be with her mother.

From the time Marge was picked up from the airport, she was anxious to get to the hospital. Her Aunt Faith took her over to her Aunt Edith's house and they didn't seem to be in a big hurry to get to the hospital. Although Letta was still in a coma, her condition had improved so there didn't seem to be any great necessity to rush. However, on the flight up to Washington, Marge had asked God to reveal to her if this would be the time 'before Christmas' as He had told her mother earlier in the year. He dropped Psalm 73:24 into her heart. As she turned in her Bible to read it, tears sprang to her eyes.

"With Thy counsel Thou wilt guide me, and afterwards receive me to glory."

She closed the Bible knowing in her heart that this would be the day her mother would be received into glory. Because of this she felt such a strong need to get to the hospital to be with her mother during her last moments on earth.

Harold was standing by his mother's side. He knew Marge was rushing to get to the hospital. He prayed, "Oh Lord, please allow Margie to be able to see Mama alive just one last time."

Finally Marge arrived at the hospital. She wasted no time going to see her mom. She pushed opened the door and the first thing she saw was her mother hooked up to some machines.

"Mama!" She cried as she rushed forward to her mother's side.

Letta lay there in a coma. Her breathing was labored. Marge looked over at Harold and saw that he knew the time was short. Looking down at her mother again, Marge saw that Letta's breathing was becoming more and more difficult. She struggled for one last breath. Those in the room could hear the infamous death rattle coming from her throat, and in the next moment she was gone.

The family agreed that Letta should be taken down to California and buried next to her husband, Rev. Harold Hansen Sr. A dark cloud hovered over the family as they stood at the gravesite. Suddenly the cloud split in two and a bright light shone directly down onto the casket. It was so spectacular that the funeral director was moved to tears. He came up to the family and told them he had never in all his years seen such a thing. He requested that he be allowed to donate funds to a memorial tent fund. The tent that was purchased with the funds collected was used to do evangelism up and down the Malayan Peninsula. As a result of the meetings held, hundreds of people came to know the Lord and went on to live for Him. Even through her death Letta was able to help bring many souls into the kingdom of heaven.

Letta T. Hansen went to be with Jesus on October 9, 1965. She was 67 years old. Throughout her life she had dedicated every day to God. He directed her path and led her each step of the way. Her time on earth had come to an end. Her earthly body was laid to rest, but her legacy would continue on.

Her daughter, Marge and her husband Fred Seaward, went back to Singapore and continued ministering there up into the new millennium. In August 2019, Fred and Marge Seaward were flown to Florida where they were honored for being the longest serving Assemblies of God Missionaries still on the field. They had served in Malaysia and Singapore for 64 years. A few months later Fred went to be with the Lord on October 6, 2019,

Fred and Margaret Belle Seaward in 2018

Marge continued to stay on ministering in Singapore.

In 2020, when the global pandemic Coronavirus disease (COVID-19) hit, instead of Marge slowing down she found herself busier than ever; preaching via live stream, teaching on Zoom classes and ministering through pre-recorded sermons which went out all over the world.

Each of Letta's grandchildren grew up to serve God, some of them working in the mission field just like their grandmother had done. Those who remained in the United States served God wholeheartedly whereever they were.

Just as Letta's vision had shown her, Marge's daughter Pam took up the post her grandmother had left behind. She set out as a single missionary at the age of twenty and journeyed far from family and friends to the Himalayan region. She raised the banner high and continued to move forward for Jesus.

Her grandson Jon Hansen and his family went to be missionaries to Kenya. They raised up leaders in this nation to continue their work. Later God called Jon to the nations to speak forth words of prophecy to world leaders.

Her grandson, Jim Hansen, and his family opened up their hearts to serve God in South America. Despite a long battle with brain cancer, he never gave up his desire to go out and serve God. In 2006, Jim went to be with His Lord and Savior. His sons, Jordan and Justin, were determined to carry the baton that their father had passed on to them. Jordan Hansen is the senior pastor of Newport Mesa Church, in California. Justin Hansen is the senior pastor of Tri-County Assembly in Ohio.

Letta Hansen's grandson, Rick Seaward, went back to Singapore to serve as a missionary. God allowed him to start a mighty mission church. Through that church, many churches were planted all over the world.

One of their main endeavors was reaching into the very heart of China. The tremendous burden God had given to Letta for those in China had not been forgotten. Before Rick Seaward went to be with the Lord in March 2018, he had handed over his baton to his son, Jeremy Seaward, who continues to lead the great mission's minded church in Singapore.

Letta's other grandson, Douglas Seaward, went to be a missionary in the land of India. Her granddaughter, Connie Ong, went to Ghana, West Africa with her husband and children to do the Lord's work. Her granddaughter Debbie Morris attached herself to a Chinese congregation in the Tulsa area and through the church she continued to reach out to the Chinese people that her grandmother had loved so much. No matter where they served the Lord, each one carried with them the spiritual heritage that Letta had planted in their lives during her lifetime.

All of her descendants can join with the psalmist in proclaiming:

"The Lord is the portion of my inheritance and my cup, Thou dost support my lot. The lines have fallen to me in pleasant places; indeed, my heritage is beautiful to me." Psalm 16:5, 6

Lois, Gwen, Harold and Margaret

Fred and Margaret Seaward with extended family, being honored, in Orlando, Florida at Assemblies of God Conference